U.S. Fish & Wildlife Service

Status and Trends of Wetlands in the Conterminous United States 2004 to 2009

I0434736

Report to Congress

Status and Trends of Wetlands in the Conterminous United States 2004 to 2009

T. E. Dahl
U.S. Fish and Wildlife Service
Fisheries and Habitat Conservation
Washington, D.C.

Acknowledgments

Many agencies, organizations, and individuals have contributed to the completion of this study. The author would like to specifically recognize the following individuals for their contributions: From the Fish and Wildlife Service, Bryan Arroyo, Assistant Director, Fisheries and Habitat Conservation; Jeff Underwood, Deputy Assistant Director, Fisheries and Habitat Conservation; David J. Stout, Chief, Division of Habitat and Resource Conservation; Robin NimsElliott, Deputy Chief, Division of Habitat and Resource Conservation; and Martin Kodis, Chief, Branch of Resource and Mapping Support[1]. Editorial, administrative and outreach assistance was provided by Cheryl Amrani and Jo Ann Mills, U.S. Fish and Wildlife Service, Arlington, VA.

A Fish and Wildlife Service Technical Review Team was responsible for ensuring the validity of standard operating procedures, appropriate implementation of technological advances and adaptations, review of source materials, project documentation and quality assurance plans. This Technical Team was composed of the following individuals: Jim Dick, Regional Wetland Coordinator, Albuquerque, NM; Jerry Tande, Regional Wetland Coordinator, Anchorage, AK; Bill Kirchner, Regional Wetland Coordinator, Portland, OR.

Key personnel from the U.S. Fish and Wildlife Service, National Standards and Support Team, Madison, WI, contributed greatly to this effort. Special acknowledgement goes to Mitchell T. Bergeson, Geographic Information Systems Specialist; Andrew Cruz, Information Technology Specialist; and Jane Harner, Geographic Information Analyst.

Additional support and assistance for field operations and analysis was provided by John Swords, Regional Wetland Coordinator, Atlanta, GA; Bill Pearson and Drew Rollman of the Alabama Ecological Services Field Office, Daphne, AL; Audrey Wilson, U.S. Fish and Wildlife Service, Albuquerque, NM.

Close cooperation with the U.S. Environmental Protection Agency, Office of Wetlands, Oceans and Watersheds, Wetlands Division has been instrumental. David Evans, Lynda Hall, Michael E. Scozzafava, Myra Price, Gregg Serenbetz, Elizabeth Riley and Chris Faulkner have generously contributed their time and expertise to this study.

Assistance from the U.S. Geological Survey has been provided by James M. (Mike) Duncan and the staff of the Commercial Partnerships Team, National Geospatial Technical Operations Center, Rolla, MO; Gary Latzke, Interagency Liaison, Wisconsin Water Science Center, Middleton, WI; and Michelle Greenwood, Reports Specialist, USGS Wisconsin Water Science Center, Middleton, WI.

Review and assistance also was provided by Lauren B. McNamara, Office of Environment and Energy, U.S. Department of Housing and Urban Development, Washington, D.C.

---

[1] Currently Deputy Chief, Division of Congressional and Legislative Affairs, U.S. Fish and Wildlife Service.

Statistical oversight and programming was done by Dr. Kenneth Burnham, Statistician, Colorado Cooperative Fish and Wildlife Research Unit, Department of Statistics, Colorado State University, Fort Collins, CO.

Peer review of the manuscript was provided by the following subject matter experts: Dr. Mary Kentula, U.S. Environmental Protection Agency, National Health and Environmental Effects Research Laboratory, Western Ecology Division, Corvallis, OR; Dr. Daniel Hubbard, Department of Wildlife and Fisheries Sciences, South Dakota State University, Brookings, SD; Dr. Ralph Morgenweck, Senior Science Advisor, U.S. Fish and Wildlife Service[2]; Susan-Marie Stedman, National Oceanic and Atmospheric Administration, National Marine Fisheries Service-Office of Habitat Conservation, Silver Spring, MD; Dr. N. Scott Urquhart, Research Scientist, Department of Statistics, Colorado State University[3], Fort Collins, CO; Dr. Bill O. Wilen, U.S. Fish and Wildlife Service, Arlington, VA; Josh Collins, Lead Scientist, San Francisco Estuary Institute, Oakland, CA; and Cherie L. Hagen, Wetland Team Leader & Policy Coordinator, Wisconsin Department of Natural Resources, Spooner, WI.

This report is the culmination of technical collaboration and partnerships. A more complete listing of some of the cooperators appears in Appendix A.

This report should be cited as follows:

Dahl, T.E. 2011. Status and trends of wetlands in the conterminous United States 2004 to 2009. U.S. Department of the Interior; Fish and Wildlife Service, Washington, D.C. 108 pp.

---

[2] Currently Scientific Integrity Officer, Department of the Interior.

[3] Retired.

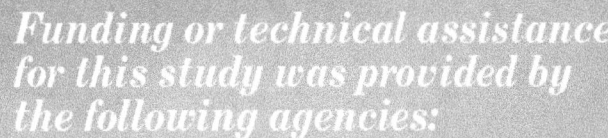

Funding or technical assistance for this study was provided by the following agencies:

Environmental Protection Agency

Department of the Army
Army Corps of Engineers —

Department of Agriculture
Natural Resources Conservation Service

Department of Commerce
National Oceanic and Atmospheric Administration
National Marine Fisheries Services

Department of the Interior
Fish and Wildlife Service

Photograph by A. Cruz, USFWS

Preface

Members of Congress:

I am pleased to provide the U.S. Fish and Wildlife Service's (Service) Status and Trends of Wetlands in the Conterminous United States 2004 to 2009 (Report) to Congress on the status and trends of our Nation's wetland resources. The Service prepared the Report after a two year study period and a rigorous statistical analysis and peer review. The Service is the principal Federal agency that provides information to the public on the extent and status of the Nation's wetlands and it works with partner organizations to maintain an active Federal role in monitoring wetland habitats of the Nation. This Report is the latest in a continuous series spanning 50 years of wetland data. It represents the most comprehensive and contemporary effort to track wetlands resources on a national scale.

While I am heartened to note that the Nation is making important progress in the conservation of our wetland resources, there is also reason for concern and continued diligence. Findings from this study indicate that between 2004 and 2009, wetland losses outdistanced wetland gains. The reasons for these changes are complex but they serve as a warning signal that additional work is needed to protect wetland resources. In 2009, I cosigned a letter emphasizing the importance of the Clean Water Act and its ramifications to the waters of the United States including wetlands.

While we have made tremendous strides, it is apparent that we continue to face challenges and wetlands continue to face pressure(s) from the effects of sea level rise, changes in climate, competing demands for natural resources, and the cumulative effects of an array of environmental stressors. The oil spill in the Gulf of Mexico has reminded us of the importance that our wetland resources play in maintaining environmental quality, habitat for fish, and wildlife species, as well as supporting social and economic pillars for the American people.

This report does not draw conclusions regarding trends in the quality of the Nation's wetlands. The Status and Trends Study collects data on wetland acreage gains and losses, as it has for the past 50 years. However, the information contained in this and previous reports have provided a context for the examination of wetland condition. The process for such an examination is already underway and the information contained in this report should be viewed as the initial step in Federal partnerships. The Administration is committed to working with governmental, corporate, and private partnerships to secure and conserve our treasured landscapes.

Ken Salazar,
Secretary, Department of the Interior

Conversion Table

U.S. Customary to Metric

inches (in.)	×	25.40	=	millimeters (mm)
inches (in.)	×	2.54	=	centimeters (cm)
feet (ft)	×	0.30	=	meters (m)
miles (mi)	×	1.61	=	kilometers (km)
square feet (ft²)	×	0.09	=	square meters (m²)
square miles (mi²)	×	2.59	=	square kilometers (km²)
acres (A)	×	0.40	=	hectares (ha)
Fahrenheit degrees (°F)	→	0.556 (°F – 32)	=	Celsius degrees (°C)

Metric to U.S. Customary

millimeters (mm)	×	0.04	=	inches (in.)
centimeters (cm)	×	0.39	=	feet (ft)
meters (m)	×	3.28	=	feet (ft)
kilometers (km)	×	0.62	=	miles (mi)
square meters (m²)	×	10.76	=	square feet (ft²)
square kilometers (km²)	×	0.39	=	square miles (mi²)
hectares (ha)	×	2.47	=	acres (A)
Celsius degrees (°C)	→	1.8 (°C) + 32	=	Fahrenheit degrees (°F)

General Disclaimer

The use of trade, product, industry or firm names or products in this report is for informative purposes only and does not constitute an endorsement by the U.S. Government or the Fish and Wildlife Service.

Contents

Acknowledgments 3

Preface 7

Executive Summary 15

Introduction 17

Study Design and Procedures 19

    Study Objectives 20

    Sampling Design 24

    Types and Dates of Imagery 27

    Methods of Data Collection and Image Analysis.. 30

    Wetland Change Detection 30

    Field Verification.. 31

    Data Quality Control 31

    Statistical Analysis... 32

    Limitations... 33

    Attribution of Wetland Losses 34

Results 37

    Status of the Nation's Wetlands... 37

    National Trends, 2004 to 2009 40

    Attribution of Wetland Gain and Loss, 2004 to 2009 41

Discussion and Analysis 45

    Marine and Estuarine Wetlands 45

    Changes in Sea Level and Coastal Processes Affecting Marine and Estuarine Wetlands 54

    Freshwater Wetlands.. 59

    Additional Analysis of Recent Changes 68

    Wetland Restoration, Reestablishment, and Creation.. 71

    Potential Vulnerability of Selected Wetland Types to Climatic Changes 86

Summary 89

References Cited 91

Appendix A. Acknowledgment of Cooperators 99

Appendix B. Definitions of Habitat Categories Used by Status and Trends...................... 101

Appendix C. Physiographic Regions of the Conterminous United States as Used in This Study.............. 105

Appendix D. Estimates of Acreage by Classification and Change between 2004 and 2009........................ 106

List of Figures

Figure 1. Freshwater wetlands of Bon Secour National Wildlife Refuge, southern Alabama, 2010 19

Figure 2. Permanently flooded lakes are examples of deepwater components of the study 22

Figure 3. Borrow pits found in association with a highway interchange have filled with water 23

Figure 4. Numerous ponds and small residential lakes, including golf course ponds have been created in this rapidly developing area 23

Figure 5. An aerial image of artificially created ponds 23

Figure 6. A small sized farmed wetland about 0.1 acre (0.04 ha)..24

Figure 7. Near-shore coastal wetland included salt marsh (A), shoals (B), tidal flats (not pictured) and bars (C)..25

Figure 8. Physiographic subdivisions of South Carolina and an example of sample plot distribution allocated in proportion to the amount of wetland area as used in this study.........................26

Figure 9. Color infrared satellite imagery (GeoEye) was used to identify and classify wetlands 27

Figure 10. Spring flood waters cover both wetland and upland along the Lemonweir River, WI 28

Figure 11. Early spring, leaf off imagery helped identify small wet forested pockets as shown in this GeoEye satellite image from eastern Michigan in March 2009 29

Figure 12. Ground level view of a small wetland swale under heavy tree canopy......................................29

Figure 13. Drainage ditches visible on aerial imagery provided indicators of change 30

Figure14. States with field verification work (green) conducted between 2009 and 2010............................31

Figure 15. Earthen berms divide a farm field used in rotation with other crops for commercial rice production, Arkansas, 2010 33

Figure 16. Planted pine forest as an example of upland forested plantation, South Carolina, 2010............35

Figure 17. Status of estuarine wetland area by type, 2009..39

Figure 18. Status of freshwater wetland area by type, 2009 39

Figure 19. Average annual net loss and gain estimates for the conterminous United States, 1954 to 2009 40

Figure 20. Estimated average annual loss of vegetated freshwater wetland area, 1974 to 2009 41

Figure 21. Percent occurrence of freshwater pond types, 2009 41

Figure 22. Estimated net gains and losses of wetland acres attributed to the various upland land use categories and deepwater, 2004 to 2009...42

Figure 23. Loss of freshwater forested wetland as attributed to upland and deepwater categories, 2004 to 2009 42

Figure 24. Wetland losses attributed to "other" landuse indicated the land may be in transition from one land use to another and the final land use type cannot be determined 43

Figure 25. This temporarily flooded wetland has reestablished naturally on lands that were part of an agricultural program set-aside 43

Figure 26. Estuarine salt marsh wetland, Florida, 2010..46

Figure 27. The attribution of estuarine emergent losses between 2004 and 2009.....................................47

Figure 28. Oil and gas field development located in estuarine wetlands of southern Louisiana..................47

Figure 29. Comparison of aerial images from 2004 and 2009 showing areas of estuarine marsh along the northern Texas coast...48

Figure 30. An example of shoreline protection measures along the coast of southeastern Louisiana 49

Figure 31. Man-made structures in areas of former estuarine marsh in southern Louisiana 50

Figure 32. Mangrove shrub wetlands along the west coast of Florida 51

Figure 33. Estimated percent area of intertidal non-vegetated wetland along the Pacific coastline of Washington, Oregon and California compared to the coastline of the Atlantic and Gulf of Mexico, 2009 52

Figure 34. The fishing pier on Dauphin Island, Alabama no longer reaches the water line as coastal sediments have been deposited along this shore (2010)...53

Figures 35 A and B. Sea birds rest and feed on intertidal habitats such as beaches and tidal flats 53

Figure 36. Beached oil from the Deepwater Horizon oil spill, 2010 54

Figure 37. Cliffs and rocky shorelines along California's Pacific coastline restrict any possible migration (retreat) of coastal wetlands as sea levels rise 55

Figure 38. Shoreline armoring and stabilization along this beach in North Carolina was designed to protect coastal dunes and development 55

Figure 39. Eroding shoreline along the Atlantic coast in Georgia...56

Figure 40. Estuarine shoreline along the northwestern Florida coast illustrated the effects of erosion and confinement of coastal plants to a narrow beach-line 57

Figure 41. Acreage immigration and emigration of freshwater emergent wetland, 2004 to 2009 61

Figure 42. Gains and losses of selected wetland, upland and deepwater categories that influenced a net gain of freshwater shrub wetland 2004 to 2009 62

Figure 43. A freshwater shrub wetland composed of true shrub species, Tennessee 63

Figure 44. Long-term trends in freshwater shrub net changes, 1974 to 2009..................................63

Figure 45. Long-term trends in forested wetland area as measured since the 1950s 64

Figure 46. Minor drainage and the installation of ditches have been considered a normal silviculture activity in wetlands designed to "temporarily dewater" a wetland 65

Figure 47. Both long-leaf (Pinus palustris) and slash pine (*Pinus elliottii*) occur naturally in southern wetlands 66

Figure 48. A former forested wetland in South Carolina one year following clear-cut 67

Figure 49. This study found particular regions of the conterminous United States experienced different rates of wetland loss depending on many factors 69

Figures 50 A. Originally, approximately 93 percent of the land area pictured was vegetated wetland with level, poorly drained or very poorly drained hydric soils (NRCS 2010) typical of the sloughs and wet flatwoods of south Florida (Liudahl et al. 1989)...70

Figure 50 B. Updated loss information showing cumulative wetland losses 1998 to 2004 and 2004 to 2009..70

Figure 51. Remnant cypress (*Taxodium sp.*) remain as part of a former forested wetland complex in south Florida 71

Figure 52. This series of image maps illustrate the end result of a 121 acre (49.0 ha) wetland reestablishment project in southern Wisconsin 75

Figure 53. Former aquaculture ponds in west-central Mississippi supported wetland emergent plant growth in 2009..77

Figure 54. A created pond in an urban subdivision has been used to drain an adjacent vegetated wetland and serves as a retention basin to compensate for the increase in impervious surface from the development...77

Figure 55. Distribution of created ponds in the conterminous United States 78

Figure 56. Many created wetlands share common characteristics of a deeper open-water basin ringed by a band of emergent vegetation 79

List of Tables

Table 1. Wetland, deepwater, and upland categories used to conduct the wetland status and trends study 21

Table 2. Change in wetland area for selected wetland and deepwater categories, 2004 to 2009 38

Table 3. Status and changes to intertidal marine and estuarine wetlands, 2004 to 2009 46

Table 4. Status and changes in freshwater wetland types between 2004 to 2009 59

Table 5. Wetland types identified in this study exhibiting change in extent or distribution from climatic conditions 87

Executive Summary

This study examined recent trends in wetland extent and habitat type throughout the conterminous United States between 2004 and 2009. Wetland trends were measured by the examination of remotely sensed imagery for 5,042 randomly selected sample plots. This imagery in combination with field verification provided a scientific basis for analysis of the extent of wetlands and changes that had occurred over the four and half year time span in this study.

This information provides a quantitative measure of the areal extent of all wetlands, regardless of ownership, in the conterminous United States. Wetlands were defined using biological criteria and standardized nomenclature for the classification of wetland types. Recently acquired remotely sensed imagery was used as the principle means to assess wetland change with a number of geoprocessing and quality control measures implemented to ensure data completeness and accuracy. The spatial sample design involved randomized sampling of geospatial information on 4.0 mi^2 (10.4 km^2) plots. This was a well-established, time-tested procedure that provided a practical, scientific approach for measuring wetland area extent (status) and change rates (trends) in the conterminous United States. Statistical estimates provided national status and change information as well as estimates by major wetland type. Field verification was completed for 898

(18 percent) of the sample plots during 2009 to 2010. Field sites were dispersed in portions of 42 States.

Enhancements to this study included augmentation to the number of sample plots along the Pacific coast of Washington, Oregon and California. This augmentation was done to provide estimates of estuarine and marine wetlands not included in the original sample design and provide a more complete estimate for these wetland types nationally.

Because of the increased area of created freshwater ponds in recent years, additional descriptive categorization for freshwater ponds was developed and implemented as part of this study. Further categorization of the physical and ecological characteristics of freshwater ponds was intended to provide information about what types of ponds have been created over time.

This report did not draw conclusions regarding trends in the quality or condition of the Nation's wetlands, but rather it provided data regarding trends in wetland extent and type and provided baseline information to facilitate ongoing collaborative efforts to assess wetland condition. Further examination of wetland condition on the national level has been initiated by the Environmental Protection Agency in conjunction with the Fish and Wildlife Service and other Federal, State and Tribal partners.

The study indicated that there were an estimated 110.1 million acres (44.6 million ha) of wetlands in the conterminous United States in 2009[4] (the coefficient of variation of the national estimate was 2.7 percent). An estimated 95 percent of all wetlands were freshwater and 5 percent were in the marine or estuarine (saltwater) systems. With the exception of minor statistical adjustments to the area estimates, the overall percentage of wetland area and representation by saltwater and freshwater components remained unchanged.

Estuarine emergent (salt marsh) wetland was the most prevalent type of all estuarine and marine intertidal wetland. Salt marsh made up an estimated 66.7 percent of all estuarine and marine wetland area. Forested wetlands made up the single largest category (49.5 percent) of wetland in the freshwater system. Freshwater emergents made up an estimated 26.3 percent, shrub wetlands 17.8 percent and freshwater ponds 6.4 percent by area.

The difference in the national estimates of wetland acreage between 2004 and 2009 was not statistically significant. Wetland area declined by an estimated 62,300 acres (25,200 ha) between 2004 and 2009. The reasons for this are complex and potentially reflect economic conditions, land use trends, changing wetland regulation and enforcement measures and climatic changes. Certain types of wetland exhibited declines while others increased in area. The result of these gains and losses yielded the net change and it was possible to have losses or gains of particular wetland types that exceed the overall net change for all wetlands.

Collectively, marine and estuarine intertidal wetlands declined by an estimated 84,100 acres (34,050 ha) or an estimated 1.4 percent between 2004 and 2009. The majority of these losses (73 percent) were to deepwater bay bottoms or open-ocean. Losses of estuarine emergent (salt marsh) and changes in marine and estuarine non-vegetated wetlands reflected the impacts of coastal storms and relative sea level rise along the coastlines of the Atlantic and Gulf of Mexico. The majority (99 percent) of all estuarine emergent losses were associated with processes related to the marine environment such as saltwater inundation and/or coastal storm events. The effects of sea level on wetlands are subject to considerable uncertainties; however, recent changes in non-vegetated intertidal wetlands (beaches, bars and shoals) along the South Atlantic and Gulf of Mexico indicated considerable instability and change. Coastal environments continue to face a variety of stressors that can interact with climate-related processes and potentially increase the vulnerability of coastal wetlands.

Overall, freshwater wetlands realized a slight increase in area between 2004 and 2009. Freshwater ponds have continued to increase although the rate of pond development had slowed from previous reporting periods. Freshwater vegetated wetlands continued to decline albeit at a reduced rate. This most recent annual rate of loss represented a reduction in the loss rate of roughly 50 percent since 2004. Declines in freshwater forested wetland area (633,100 acres or 256,300 ha) negated area gains in freshwater emergent and shrub categories.

Forested wetlands sustained their largest losses since the 1974 to 1985 time period. Freshwater wetland losses continued in regions of the country where there has been potential for wetlands to come into conflict with competing land and resource development interests.

Between 2004 and 2009, 489,600 acres (198,230 ha) of former upland were re-classified as wetland. These increases were attributed to wetland reestablishment and creation on agricultural lands and other uplands with undetermined land use including undeveloped land, lands in conservation programs or idle lands. The rate of wetland reestablishment increased by an estimated 17 percent from the previous study period (1998 and 2004). Conversely, the estimated wetland loss rate increased 140 percent during the same time period and, as a consequence, national wetland losses have outdistanced gains.

The cumulative effects of losses in the freshwater system have had consequences for hydrologic and ecosystem connectivity. In certain regions, profound reductions in wetland extent have resulted in habitat loss, fragmentation, and limited opportunities for reestablishment and watershed rehabilitation.

---

[4] This estimate has been revised to reflect 2010 wetland status as well as the addition of wetland area in the coastal zone of the Pacific coast for WA, OR, and CA as described in the Sample Design section of this report.

Introduction

The mission of the U.S. Fish and Wildlife Service (Service) is to conserve, protect, and enhance fish, wildlife, plants, and their habitats for the continuing benefit of the American people. The Service has been entrusted with legal authorities and responsibilities for fish and wildlife conservation including the management of fish and wildlife populations; conserving endangered and threatened species, inter-jurisdictional fish, and migratory birds; managing an extensive conservation land base; and collaborating in carrying out conservation activities under international conventions, treaties, and agreements. The Service communicates information essential for public awareness and understanding of the importance of fish and wildlife resources and changes reflecting environmental conditions that ultimately will affect the welfare of people.

Wetlands are transitional from true aquatic habitats to dry land (upland) and as a result, their abundance, type, and condition are directly reflected in the health and abundance of many species. In 1986, the United States Congress enacted the Emergency Wetlands Resources Act (Public Law 99-645) recognizing that wetlands are nationally important resources and that these resources have been affected by human activities. Under the provisions of this Act, the Service is required to update wetland status and trends studies of the Nation's wetlands at 10 year intervals. To date, there have been five national reports on wetland status with this study being the latest. Recently, Congress has considered a number of policy issues that involve wetlands. Some of these reflect long-standing interests of the Federal government and influence a number of incentive and disincentive measures to conserve wetlands and if possible increase both the extent and improve the environmental quality aspects wetlands provide (Copeland 2010). This study tracks and quantifies wetland losses, reestablishment (restoration) or creation and provides a *measureable element* to gauge Federal policy success and provide information crucial to understanding this important resource type.

There has been keen interest in wetland trends since the Supreme Court decisions in 2001 and 2006 that narrowed the interpretation of the scope of waters and wetlands protected by the Clean Water Act[5]. Previous information on wetland trends pre-dated the 2006 Rapanos and Carabell decisions (Rapanos v. United States and Carabell v. United States) and changes in the wetland regulatory process. The Supreme Court decisions narrowed the prior interpretation of the scope of waters protected under the Clean Water Act and agencies have faced challenges implementing those decisions (Council on Environmental Quality 2009). The effects of those decisions are reflected in the data collected between 2004 and 2009 and reported here.

---

[5] The 1977 amendments, the Clean Water Act of 1977 [P.L. 95-217].

Since 2004, several severe hurricanes have struck the coastline along the Gulf of Mexico and these data afford an indication of wetland area changes sustained as a result of those storms.

In addition, the wetland extent information presented in this report has important uses by resource managers as they interpret the role of wetlands on the national landscape. This study was designed to provide scientific information to resource specialists and decision makers about wetlands resource trends. These data help guide decisions on wetland-related issues, such as reestablishment and enhancement, endangered species habitat availability, possible changes resulting from climatic change, strategic habitat conservation, and ecosystem management planning. Wetland status and trends data continue to be used extensively by Federal, State, local and Tribal governments to develop wetland conservation strategies, strategic management actions, and validate performance toward halting loss and reestablishing wetlands.

The goals of this study were to:

- Describe the resource type, extent, trends and reporting the results for the Nation through time;

- Maintain survey integrity and avoid bias;

- Provide relevant, contemporary data to aid in assessment or formulation of policy;

- Establish high standards for data quality; and update procedures to incorporate new and proven technologies and enhancements.

In 2004, the Service's Wetlands Status and Trends data indicated that for the first time there had been a net increase in wetland area (estimated gain of 32,000 acres or 12,900 ha) between 1998 and 2004; however, qualitative aspects of wetlands remained unknown. Since 2000, observed changes in wetland type(s) and the continued loss of freshwater vegetated wetlands coupled with increases in freshwater ponds have raised questions regarding the ecological integrity of the existing wetlands. As more comprehensive assessment of wetland condition has become a higher priority for Federal agencies, this study has contributed relevant data on wetland type, location, and extent to be used as part of the first national wetland condition assessment currently being conducted by the Environmental Protection Agency (EPA). The Service has worked closely with EPA in preparation for the National Wetland Condition Assessment Study scheduled to be released in 2013. The two agencies have been collaborating on a number of technical monitoring and data collection efforts. The potential outcome of these studies on wetland quantity and quality will assist in further assessment of wetland status and efficacy of programs and policies.

The Service has continued to work closely with other key partner organizations and this multi-agency involvement has enhanced the wetlands status and trends study design, data collection, verification, peer review and data applications to address challenges of resource

management, research and policy formulation. In 2009, collaboration with the National Oceanic and Atmospheric Administration (NOAA–Fisheries), produced a report based on further analysis of the 1998 to 2004 national status and trends information for the coastal watersheds of the Atlantic, Gulf of Mexico, and Great Lakes. The results of that effort indicated that coastal watersheds were losing wetlands despite the national trend of net gains, and pointed to the need for an expanded effort on conservation of wetlands in those coastal watersheds. These findings have stimulated subsequent actions from agencies addressing the need for further policy considerations and focused conservation measures in those coastal areas.

Continued monitoring of wetland resources has been widely considered essential for identifying changes in the wetland community type, spatial extent, and guiding additional research or management actions. This information combined with historical perspectives increase our understanding of landscape patterns and processes.

Study Design
and Procedures

Figure 1. Freshwater wetlands of
Bon Secour National Wildlife Refuge,
southern Alabama, 2010.

Study Objectives

This study was designed to provide the Nation with current, scientifically valid information on the status and extent of wetland resources and to measure change in those resources over time. It is a quantitative measure of the areal extent of all wetlands, regardless of ownership, in the conterminous United States and provides no indication of wetland quality outside of the changes in wetland area, by category.

Wetland Definition and Classification

During the mid-1970s, the Fish and Wildlife Service began work on a biological definition of wetland and standardized nomenclature for the classification of wetland types. This system described by Cowardin *et al.* (1979) was adopted as a standard by the Service and subsequently became a Federal Geographic Data Committee (FGDC) Standard for mapping, monitoring, and reporting on wetlands (FGDC 1996). This institutionalization of a biological definition and classification system has facilitated its use in each of the national wetland status and trends studies and has provided consistency and continuity by defining the biological extent of wetlands and common descriptors for wetland types.

This study continued the use of the Cowardin *et al.* (1979) definition of wetland. It is a two-part definition as indicated below:

Wetlands are lands transitional between terrestrial and aquatic systems where the water table is usually at or near the surface or the land is covered by shallow water.

For purposes of this classification, wetlands must have one or more of the following three attributes: (1) at least periodically, the land supports predominantly hydrophytes, (2) the substrate is predominantly undrained hydric soil, and (3) the substrate is nonsoil and is saturated with water or covered by shallow water at some time during the growing season of each year.

Cowardin *et al.* (1979) and other researchers (Gosselink and Turner 1978; Mitsch and Gosselink 1993) recognized that hydrology was universally regarded as the most basic feature of wetlands and that hydrology, not the presence of vegetation, determines the existence of wetland (Cowardin and Golet 1995). For this reason, in areas that lack vegetation or soils (e.g., mud flats, sand or gravel bars, and shorelines), hydrology determines that these areas are wetlands.

Table 1. Wetland, deepwater, and upland categories used to conduct the wetland status and trends study. The definitions for each category appear in Appendix B.

Salt Water Habitats	Common Description
Marine Subtidal*	Open Ocean
Marine Intertidal	Near shore
Estuarine Subtidal*	Open-water/bay bottoms
Estuarine Intertidal Emergents	Salt marsh
Estuarine Intertidal Forested/Shrub	Mangroves or other estuarine shrubs
Estuarine Intertidal Unconsolidated Shore	Beaches/bars
Riverine* (may be tidal or non-tidal)	River systems

Freshwater Habitats	
Palustrine Forested	Forested swamps
Palustrine Shrub	Shrub wetlands
Palustrine Emergents	Inland marshes/wet meadows
Palustrine Farmed	Farmed wetlands
Palustrine Unconsolidated Bottom (ponds)	Open-water ponds/aquatic bed
Pond – Natural characteristics	Small bog lakes, vernal pools, kettles, beaver ponds, alligator holes
Pond – Industrial	Flooded mine or excavation sites (including highway borrow sites), in-ground treatment ponds or lagoons, holding ponds
Pond – Urban use	Aesthetic or recreational ponds, golf course ponds, residential lakes, ornamental ponds, water retention ponds
Pond – Agriculture use	Ponds in proximity to agricultural, farming or silviculture operations such as farm ponds, dug outs for livestock, agricultural waste ponds, irrigation or drainage water retention ponds
Pond - Aquaculture	Ponds singly or in series used for aquaculture including cranberries, fish rearing
Lacustrine*	Lakes and reservoirs

Uplands	
Agriculture	Cropland, pasture, managed rangeland
Urban	Cities and incorporated developments
Forested Plantations	Planted or intensively managed forests; silviculture
Rural Development	Non-urban developed areas and infrastructure
Other Uplands	Rural uplands not in any other category; barren lands

*Constitutes deepwater habitat

Ephemeral waters[6], which are not recognized as a wetland type, and certain types of "farmed wetlands" as defined by the Food Security Act were not included in this study because they do not meet the Cowardin *et al.* definition. Habitat category definitions including the latest categorization of freshwater ponds developed for this study are given in synoptic form in Table 1. Complete definitions of wetland types and land use categories used in this study are provided in Appendix B.

Deepwater Habitats

Wetlands and deepwater habitats are defined separately by Cowardin *et al.* (1979) because the term wetland does not include deep, permanent water bodies. Deepwater habitats are permanently flooded land lying below the deepwater boundary of wetlands (Figure 2). Deepwater habitats include environments where surface water is permanent and often deep, so that water, rather than air, is the principal medium in which the dominant organisms live, whether or not they are attached to the substrate. For the purposes of conducting status and trends work, all lacustrine (lake) and riverine (river) waters were considered deepwater habitats.

Upland Categories

Upland included lands not meeting the definition of either wetland or deepwater habitats. An abbreviated upland classification system patterned after the U. S. Geological Survey land classification scheme described by Anderson *et al.* (1976), with five generalized categories, was used to describe uplands in this study. These upland categories as well as all other wetland and deepwater categories are listed in Table 1.

[6] This refers to temporary surface water and should not be confused with ephemeral (temporary) wetlands.

Figure 2. Permanently flooded lakes are examples of deepwater components of the study (Jackson Lake, Wyoming, 2010).

Addition of Descriptive Categories for Freshwater Ponds

This study was designed as a scientific approach to monitor the Nation's wetlands using a consistent, biological definition. Cowardin *et al.* (1979) recognized ponds as an important component of the aquatic ecosystem and included them within a larger system of freshwater wetlands. This classification system for wetlands became a Service Standard (USFWS 1980) as well as the FGDC standard for monitoring and reporting on wetlands (FGDC 1996). Open water ponds have been included in every wetland status and trends report conducted by the Service using the Cowardin *et al.* classification system. These past studies have provided a quantitative measure of the areal extent of all wetlands in the conterminous United States. Qualitative assessment of wetland function was beyond the scope of the status and trends study objectives.

Because of the proliferation of created open water ponds in recent years, there have been questions regarding the ecological implications of increasing the number and area of open water wetlands identified during the 2005 wetlands status and trends analysis. In 2006, EPA and the Service began working together to design a method for further categorizing the physical characteristics and ecological contributions of freshwater ponds on the landscape. As a result of that effort, additional descriptive categories for freshwater ponds have been added as part of this study. This information was intended to provide users with additional insight about what types and how many ponds were created over time.

Water features that have been excluded from this study as non-wetland include stock watering tanks, swimming pools, industrial waste pits, stormwater drains (non-retention features), garden ponds or fountains (coy or koi ponds), water treatment facilities, municipal or industrial water storage tanks, sewage treatment facilities (other than wetlands designed to filter effluent), water cooling towers or tanks, road culverts or ditches, and other "ephemeral" waters.

Further subdivision of freshwater ponds (palustrine unconsolidated bottom wetlands) was carefully considered to allow the re-aggregation of the data to the original classification unit (all ponds). Another important consideration was the ability to accurately determine the appropriate descriptive pond category by the use of remotely sensed imagery. Pond descriptive categories were field tested to ensure that a consistent scientific approach was implemented and the descriptive terms used would provide users with additional information about pond characteristics and numbers. Five descriptive categories of freshwater ponds were used as part of this study. These are listed below together with a brief description of characteristics and remote sensing indicators used to identify and classify these areas.

Freshwater Pond Categories: Descriptive Types

(1) **Ponds with natural features or characteristics** as indicated by lack of human modification or development. These include naturally occurring ponds, bog lakes, vernal pools, potholes, kettles, beaver ponds, alligator holes, etc.

(2) **Ponds used for industrial purposes** such as mine reclamation sites, excavated pits or mine drainage ponds, highway borrow pits (Figure 3), sewage lagoons, and other wetlands designed to filter effluent, and industrial holding ponds.

(3) **Urban ponds** built and used for aesthetics or recreational purposes such as golf course ponds, small (<20 acres) residential lakes, ornamental water bodies, water retention basins (Figure 4).

(4) **Ponds found in conjunction to agriculture, farming, or silvicultural operations** such as farm ponds, dug outs for livestock, agricultural waste ponds, irrigation or sediment retention ponds.

(5) **Aquaculture ponds** that occur singly or in series (Figure 5) and are used for some form of aquaculture including fish or shellfish rearing. Commercial cranberry growing operations also are placed in this category.

Figure 3. (Top) Borrow pits (indicated by the blue arrows) found in association with a highway interchange have filled with water (color infrared aerial image). The shape and proximity of these ponds provided good indicators for further descriptive categorization.

Figure 4. (Middle) Numerous ponds and small residential lakes (indicated by the red arrows), including golf course ponds (blue arrows) have been created in this rapidly developing area. These types of ponds were classified as "urban ponds" in this study.

Figure 5. (Bottom) An aerial image of artificially created ponds (blue and green geometric shapes). Ponds in series provided indicators of aquaculture operations such as the catfish farm shown here (Mississippi, 2009).

Sampling Design

Sample-based surveys and monitoring methods such as those used in this study have been an effective means to gather information regarding various resource types. Because continued pressures on wetland resources require effective monitoring at temporal and spatial scales that are useful for contributing to wetland conservation efforts, resource managers, researchers, and policy makers have come to rely on recent wetlands status and trends information.

This study used a practical, scientific approach for measuring wetland area extent (status) and change rates (trends) in the conterminous United States. The development of the target population for wetlands, sample frame, probabilistic sampling procedures and the recent improvements used have been described in previous reporting (Dahl 2000; 2006) and further reviewed in detail (Dahl in manuscript). The study measured wetland extent and change using a statistically stratified, simple random sampling design. The foundations and scientific principles underlying such surveys are well developed and have been applied for several iterations of national reporting. These techniques have been used to monitor conversions between ecologically different wetland types, as well as measure wetland gains and losses in area.

The essentials of survey design provide the basis for (a) selecting a subset of sampling units from which to collect data, and (b) choosing methods for analyzing the data. Olsen *et al.* (1999) have described the conceptual relationships among the key elements in a probabilistic sampling survey design. These same elements were incorporated in the design of this study as initially developed and implemented by interagency statisticians. Sample plots were examined with the use of remotely sensed imagery in combination with field reconnaissance work to determine wetland change.

Monitoring All Wetlands

To monitor changes in wetland area, the 48 conterminous States were stratified or divided by State boundaries and 35 physiographical subdivisions described by Hammond (1970) and shown in Appendix C. Habitats were identified primarily by the analysis of imagery, and wetlands were identified based on vegetation, visible hydrology, and geography. There was a margin of error inherent in the use of imagery, thus detailed on-the-ground inspection of any particular site may result in revision of the wetland boundaries or classification established through image analysis (Dahl and Bergeson 2009). The accuracy of image interpretation depended on the quality of the imagery, the experience of the image analysts, the amount and quality of the collateral data, and the amount of ground truth verification work conducted. The minimum targeted delineation size for wetlands was 1 acre (0.40 ha). Results from this and past status and trends studies indicated the minimum feature routinely delineated was about 0.1 acre (0.04 ha), but there was no assurance that all wetlands this size were detected (Figure 6).

Figure 6. A small sized farmed wetland about 0.1 acre (0.04 ha). Findings from this study indicated that wetlands smaller than 1 acre were routinely detected as part of the survey, however, there was no assurance that all wetlands less than the minimum target size were identified.

Some natural resource assessments stop at county boundaries or at a point coinciding with the census line for inhabitable land area. Doing so may exclude offshore wetlands, shallow water embayments or sounds, shoals, sand bars, tidal flats, and reefs (Figure 7). These were important resources to quantify and monitor especially in light of climatic change(s) that may result in sea level rise[7]. This study included wetlands in coastal areas by adding a supplemental sampling stratum along the coastal fringes of the conterminous United States. This stratum included the near shore areas of the coast with its barrier islands, coastal marshes, exposed tidal flats and other offshore features not a part of the landward physiographic zones.

The coastal zone stratum of the Atlantic and Gulf of Mexico included 28.2 million acres (11.4 million ha). At its widest point in southern Louisiana, this zone extended about 92.6 mi (149 km) from Lake Pontchartrain to the farthest extent of estuarine wetland resources. In this area, saltwater was the overriding influence on biological systems. The coastal zone as described in this study was not synonymous with any State or Federal jurisdictional coastal zone definitions. The legal definition of "coastal zone" has been developed for use in coastal demarcations, planning, regulatory and management activities undertaken by other Federal or State agencies.

A substantial enhancement to this study included the addition of 290 supplemental sample plots to form a coastal stratum along the Pacific coast of Washington, Oregon, and California. These plots were randomly distributed

within an additional stratum that approximated the extent of coastal watersheds. Sampling included all types of wetlands (fresh and saltwater) that were physically located within the 8-digit Hydrologic Unit Code areas (watersheds) that drained directly to the Pacific Ocean. The number of sample plots was determined by the total area within the stratum. Working in cooperation with the EPA and NOAA, this sampling stratum was incorporated as part of the national sampling effort. In the past, Pacific coast estuarine wetlands, such as those in San Francisco Bay,

California; Coos Bay, Oregon; or Puget Sound, Washington, were not extensively sampled because they occurred in discontinuous patches that precluded establishment of a coastal stratum similar to that of the Gulf and Atlantic coast (Dahl 2006). Improved geographic information systems and increased knowledge of wetland distribution allowed the Pacific coastal wetlands to be incorporated as part of this update. Augmentation was done to provide estimates of estuarine and marine wetlands not included in the original sample design and provide a more complete estimate for these wetland types nationally.

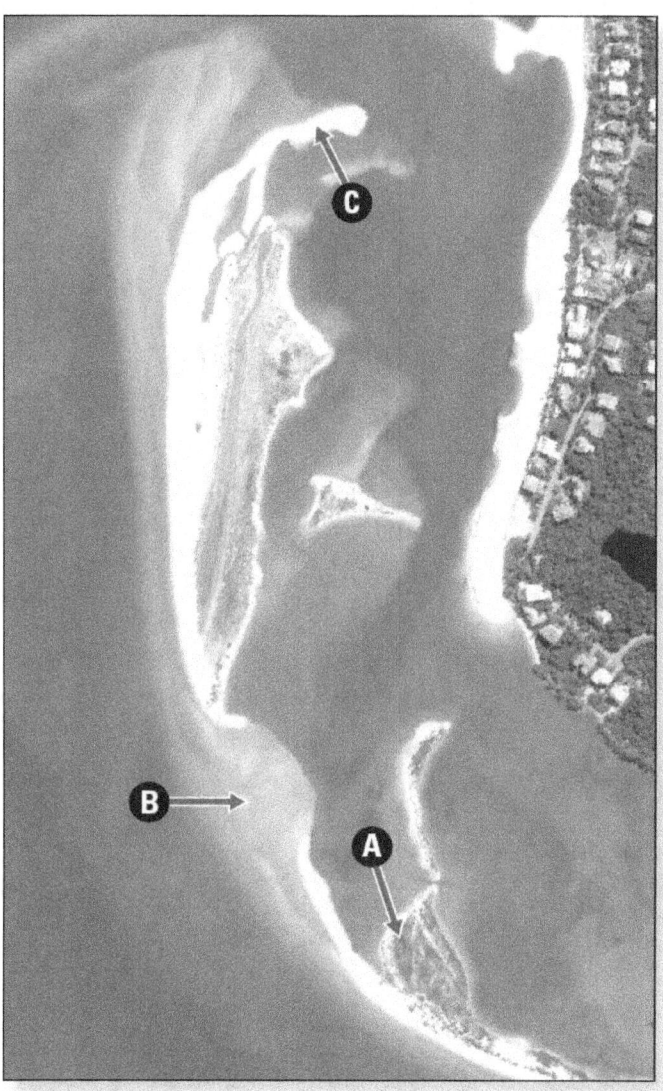

Figure 7. Near-shore coastal wetland included salt marsh (A), shoals (B), tidal flats (not pictured), and bars (C).

---

[7] Including other catastrophic events such as hurricanes and tropical storms..

To permit even spatial coverage of the sample plots, the 36 physiographic regions formed by the Hammond subdivisions and the coastal zone stratum were intersected with State boundaries to form multiple subdivisions or strata. An example of this stratification approach and how it relates to sampling intensity is shown for South Carolina (Figure 8).

Weighted, stratified sample plots were randomly allocated in proportion to the amount of wetland acreage expected to occur in each physiographic strata described above. Each sample area was a surface plot 2.0 mi (3.2 km) on a side or 4.0 mi² of area equaling 2,560 acres (1,036 ha). Plots were examined at two different time periods (2004 and 2009) to determine wetland type, extent, and change between the two periods. Stratification of the Nation based on differences in wetland density made this study an effective measure of wetland resources as it offered ecological, statistical, and practical advantages for determining wetland acreage trends and monitoring conversions between ecologically different wetland types. These plots formed a geospatially fixed, permanent sampling network. Such monitoring networks provide the advantage of measuring cumulative impacts accurately over time (Smith 2004).

Because declining wetland loss rates require finite measurement techniques to ensure a high degree of statistical reliability, the sample size of this study has been systematically augmented with additional sample plots since the late 1990s. The area analyzed in this study was comprised of 5,042 sample plots (total area equal to 20,192 mi² or 51,893 km²).

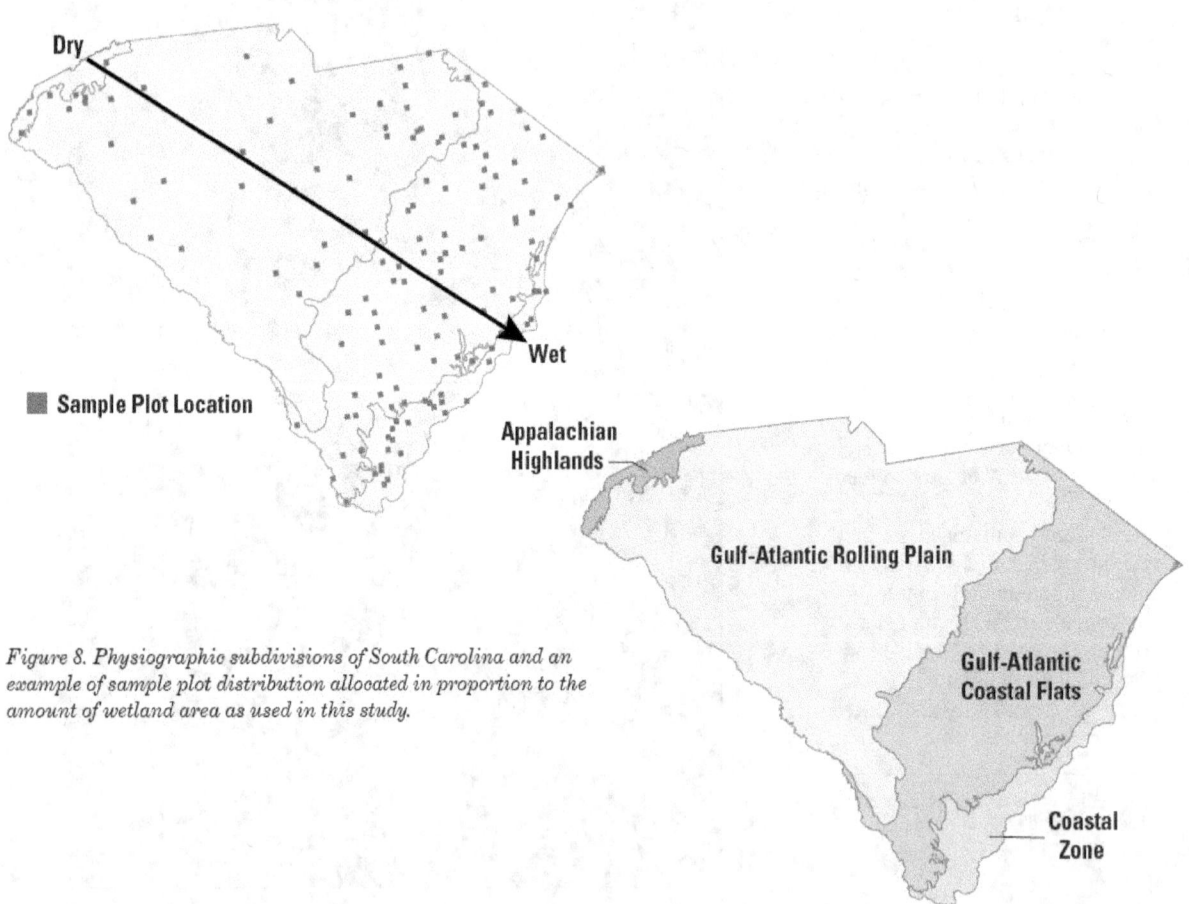

Figure 8. Physiographic subdivisions of South Carolina and an example of sample plot distribution allocated in proportion to the amount of wetland area as used in this study.

Types and Dates of Imagery

Remotely sensed imagery has become an invaluable source for ecological characterization, land cover survey, and change detection (Miller and Rogan 2007). Various commercial satellite platforms with improved spatial resolution and sensors have made detailed imagery more readily available and applicable to wetlands identification, classification, and monitoring work. The comparison of historical and recent imagery to determine change increases our understanding of natural and human-induced processes at work on the landscape (Jenson 2007).

<hr>

[s] Analysis of imagery was supplemented with substantial field work and ground observations.

In this study, image analysts relied primarily on observable physical or spectral characteristics evident on high altitude imagery, in conjunction with collateral data, to make decisions regarding wetland extent and classification[s]. Remote sensing techniques to detect and monitor wetlands in the United States and Canada have been used successfully by a number academic researchers and governmental agencies (Frohn *et al.* 2009; Jenson 2007; Dechka *et al.* 2002; Watmough *et al.* 2002; McCoy 2005; National Research Council 1995; Patience and Klemas 1993; Lillesand and Kiefer 1987). The use of remotely sensed imagery, either from aircraft or satellite, has been a cost effective way to conduct surveys over expansive areas (Dahl and Watmough 2007) and the frequency and repeatability of remotely sensed information

is invaluable for detecting and monitoring changes on the landscape (Rogan *et al.* 2002). The Fish and Wildlife Service has successfully used remote sensing techniques to determine the biological extent of wetlands for the past 35 years.

Recent imagery from multiple platforms and direct on-the-ground observations were used to determine wetland changes. Only high quality imagery was used and in some instances multiple dates of imagery were acquired to better determine wetland extent and change. To recognize and classify wetland vegetation, color infrared imagery was preferred (Figure 9).

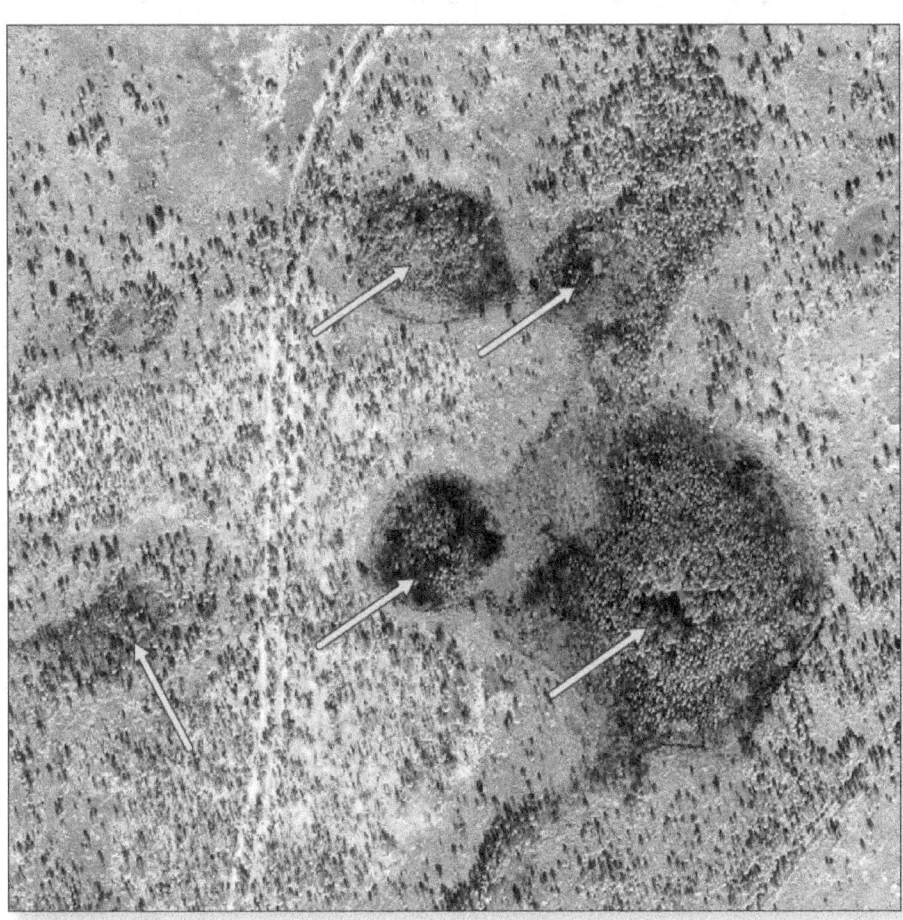

Figure 9. Color infrared satellite imagery (GeoEye) was used to identify and classify wetlands. Several wetland basins and cover types (indicated by arrows) were evident in this example from Florida, 2008.

27

Figure 10. Spring flood waters cover both wetland and upland along the Lemonweir River, WI. Extreme climatic conditions can negate the value of early spring (leaf-off) imagery intended to aid in the identification of wetland habitats.

Past studies found that leaf-off (early spring or late fall) imagery worked well to detect some types of wetlands under forested canopy; however, changes in cyclical climatic conditions are increasingly forcing reassessment of the timing of image capture in some regions. Imagery obtained when vegetation was dormant allowed for better identification of wetland boundaries as long as this timing did not coincide with seasonal flood events, drought, or wildfires that prevented accurate landscape characterization (Figure 10). For some habitat types such as forested wetlands, there have been distinct advantages to using leaf-off imagery to detect the extent of early season inundation. Under most circumstances, leaf-off imagery enhanced the visual evidence of hydrologic conditions such as saturation, flooding, or

ponding in closed canopy habitats (Figures 11 and 12). However, for other wetland types, mid-growing season may offer advantages for wetland detection. Jensen (2007) points out that the best time of imagery acquisition for detecting smooth cordgrass (*Spartina alterniflora*) in South Carolina's salt marshes was from July through October. Thus, the optimum time to obtain imagery depended on many factors including the resource extent, habitat type, and seasonal conditions. The use of additional sources of information to complement remotely sensed imagery has always been important for accurate analysis. Imagery combined with collateral data sources such as soil surveys, topographic maps, and wetland or vegetation maps were used to identify and delineate the areal extent of wetlands in this study.

Multiple sources of satellite imagery in combination with recently acquired digital photography were used to complete this study. Satellite imagery made up about 40 percent of the source imagery and offered the advantage of higher resolution digital imagery that had been acquired close to the target date. Satellite imagery was supplemented with National Agriculture Imagery Program (NAIP) imagery acquired during the agricultural growing season. NAIP and other sources of aerial imagery made up about 60 percent of the source imagery analyzed. (For technical specifications of NAIP imagery see: http://www.fsa.usda.gov/FSA/.) The mean date of the imagery used to complete this study was 2009, thus there was a 4.5 year mean differential between target dates (2004 to 2009).

Figure 11. (Top) Early spring, leaf off imagery helped identify small wet forested pockets (green arrows indicate some example areas) as shown in this GeoEye satellite image from eastern Michigan in March 2009.

Figure 12. (Bottom) Ground level view of a small wetland swale under heavy tree canopy.

Methods of Data Collection and Image Analysis

The identification of wetlands through image analysis forms the foundation for deriving all subsequent products and results. Consequently, a great deal of emphasis has been placed on the quality of the image interpretation[9]. Information on the elements of image interpretation techniques have been discussed by a number of authors (Jensen 2007; Philipson 1996; Lillesand and Kiefer 1987). Specific protocols used for image interpretation of wetlands in this study have been documented by Dahl and Bergeson (2009). Wetlands were identified based on vegetation, visible hydrology, and physical geography. Delineations on the sample plots reflected ecological change or changes in land use that influenced the size, distribution, or classification of wetland habitats.

Wetland Change Detection

Technological advances in the acquisition of remotely sensed imagery and computerized mapping techniques often provide the ability to capture more detailed information about Earth objects. The integration of Geographic Information Systems (GIS) and remote sensing for ecological monitoring has become even more important as technologies have improved and ecological assessments address more challenging issues (Miller

and Rogan 2007). The use of such technologies as part of this study provided tremendous advantages for producing higher quality natural resource information including wetland location, extent and type.

In this study, change detection and analysis involved identifying wetland gains and/or losses, cover type changes as well as upland land use changes. To determine changes between eras required the comparison of the existing sample plot information from the past era (circa 2004) to more recent imagery for the same area (circa 2009). Changes in wetland area represented realistic and logical analysis, avoiding any false or unlikely changes[10]. All change information was carefully scrutinized and verified. Examination of sites in the field or the use of collateral data assisted in this process. To ensure accuracy, the temporal dynamics of wetlands and the subtleness of many of the wetland alterations required substantial

reliance on the analysis of imagery and proper implementation of the prescribed protocols and techniques in combination with field verification.

False changes were avoided by observing positive visual evidence of a change in land use. Examples included the presence of new drainage ditches (Figure 13), canals or other man-made water courses, evidence of dredging, spoil deposition or fills, impoundments, excavations, structures, pavement or hardened surfaces, in addition to the lack of any hydrology, vegetation or soil indicators indicative of wetland. Difficulties in determining wetland change have been related to availability, timing or quality of the imagery (Watmough *et al.* 2002; Dahl 2004), and correctly interpreting wetland change has been especially challenging at times when hydrologic conditions were not optimal (i.e. drought or flooded conditions).

---

[9] The Service makes no attempt to adapt or apply the products of these techniques to regulatory or legal authorities regarding wetland boundary determinations or to jurisdiction or land ownership.

[10] An example of an unlikely change might involve upland-urban development converted to palustrine forested wetland in a short period of time (less than 5 years).

Figure 13. Drainage ditches visible on aerial imagery provided indicators of change.

Figure 14. States with field verification work (green) conducted between 2009 and 2010.

The goal of updating wetland status and trends plots was to produce data that match existing wetland and deepwater conditions (on-the-ground) as closely as possible. These data derived from the plot information reflected ecological change(s) that influenced the size, distribution, or classification of wetland habitats.

Field Verification

Field verification was completed for 898 (18 percent) of the sample plots distributed in 42 States (Figure 14).

---

[11] Results of field verification work indicated no discernible differences in the size or classification of wetlands delineated using either satellite imagery or the high altitude photography. Errors of wetland omission were 2 percent based on occurrence but less than 1 percent based on area (omitted wetlands generally were small < 1.0 acre or 0.4 ha). Errors of inclusion of upland were less than 1 percent in both occurrence and area. There was no difference regionally, between States or data analysts in the number of errors found based on field inspections, although not all plots were included in the field analysis.

Field work was done primarily as a quality control measure to verify that plot delineations were correct. Verification involved field visits to a cross section of wetland types, geographic settings, and to plots with different image types, scales and dates. Field work was not conducted in some Western States because of the remote location (limited access) and logistical problems associated with these areas. Of the 898 sample plots reviewed in the field, 28 percent used satellite imagery as the source data and 72 percent used high altitude digital photography. All field verification work took place between May 2009 and September 2010[11]. Approximately 39 percent of the total population of sample plots have had some field reconnaissance work completed within the past 10 years.

Data Quality Control

Advances in information technology and geographic information systems have influenced public expectations for greater utility and functionality from Government data sources and there has been a growing importance and sensitivity placed on data quality and integrity. To ensure the reliability of wetland status and trends data, procedural guidelines and various quality assurance and quality control measures were followed. The goal of these guidelines was to ensure that the data collection, analysis, verification and reporting methods used supported decisions for which the data were intended. Some of the major quality control steps included:

Plot Location and Positional Accuracy

Sample plots were permanently fixed georeferenced areas used to monitor land use and cover type changes. The same plot population has been re-analyzed for each status and trends report cycle. The plot coordinates were positioned precisely using a system of redundant locators in a geographic information system. Topographic maps, other maps used for collateral information and the aerial imagery were used during the study to reaffirm sample locations. All plots were also verified for the correct spatial coordinates, size and geographic projection.

Quality Control of Interpreted Images

This study used well established, time-tested, fully documented data collection and analysis procedures. To facilitate training and consistent application of data collection and quality control measures, a relatively small cadre of highly skilled and experienced personnel was used for image analysis. Image analysis was reviewed by technical expert(s) with the review consisting of adherence to geospatial data standards, ecological logic and other quality requirements.

Data Verification

All digital data files were subjected to rigorous quality control inspections. Digital data verification included quality control checks that addressed the geospatial topology, data completeness and integrity as well as some geoprocessing aspects of the data. These steps took place following the review and qualitative acceptance of the updated change information. Implementation of quality checks ensured that the data conformed to the specified criteria, thus achieving the project objectives.

Quality Assurance of Digital Data Files

There were tremendous advantages in using advanced technologies to store and analyze the geographic data. The geospatial analysis capabilities built into this study provided a complete digital database to better assist analysis of wetland change information. All digital data files were subjected to rigorous quality control inspections. Automated checking modules incorporated in the geographic information system (Arc/GIS) were used to correct digital artifacts including polygon topology. Additional customized data inspections were made to ensure that the changes indicated at the image analysis stage were properly executed. Digital file quality control reviews also provided confirmation of plot location, stratum assignment, and total land or water area sampled.

Customized digital data verification tools designed specifically for use with this sample plot work were used to check for improbable changes that may represent errors in the image interpretation. The software considered the length of time between update cycles and identified certain unrealistic cover-type changes and other types of potential errors in the data.

Statistical Analysis

The wetland status and trends study was based on a scientific probability sample of the surface area of the 48 conterminous States. The area sampled was about 1.93 billion acres (0.8 billion ha), and the sampling did not discriminate based on land ownership. The study used a stratified, simple random sampling design. Given the total possible plot population, the sampling design was stratified by use of the 36 physical subdivisions described in the "Study Design" section. Once stratified, the land subdivisions represented large areas where the samples were distributed to obtain an even spatial representation of plots. The final stratification, based on intersecting physiographic land types with State boundaries, guaranteed an improved spatial random sample of plots.

Geographic information system software organized the information for the 5,042 random sample plots. All sample plots in a stratum were given equal selection probabilities. In the data analysis phase, the adjustments were made for varying plot sizes (some lots were split by study boundaries) by use of ratio estimation theory. For any wetland type, the proportion of its area in the sample of plots in a stratum was an unbiased estimator of the unknown proportion of that type in that stratum. Inference about total wetland acreage by wetland type or for all wetlands in any stratum began with the ratio (r) of the relevant total acreage observed in the sample (Ty), for that stratum divided by the total area of the sample (Tx). Thus, y was measured in each sample plot; $r = Ty/Tx$, and the estimated total acreage of the relevant wetland type in the stratum was A x r. The sum of these estimated totals over all strata provided the national estimate for the wetland type in question. Uncertainty, which was measured as sampling variance of an estimate, was estimated based on the variation among the sample proportions in a stratum (the estimation of sample variation is highly technical and not presented here). The sampling variation of the national total was the sum of the sampling variance over all strata. These methods have been a standard for ratio estimation in association with a stratified random sampling design (Sarndal et al. 1992; Thompson 1992).

By use of this statistical procedure, the sample plot data were expanded to specific physiographic regions, by wetland type, and statistical estimates were generated for the 48 conterminous States. The reliability of each estimate generated is expressed as the percent coefficient of variation (% C.V.) associated with that estimate. Percent coefficient of variation was expressed as (standard deviation/mean) × (100).

Procedural Error

Procedural or measurement errors occur in the data collection phase of any study and must be considered. Procedural error was related to the ability to accurately recognize and classify wetlands both from multiple sources of imagery and on-the-ground evaluations. Types of procedural errors may have included missed wetlands, inclusion of

upland as wetland, misclassification of wetlands or misinterpretation of data collection protocols. The amount of introduced procedural error is usually a function of the quality of the data collection conventions; the number, variability, training and experience of data collection personnel; and the rigor of any quality control or quality assurance measures (Dahl and Bergeson 2009).

Rigorous quality control reviews and redundant inspections were incorporated into the data collection and data entry processes to help reduce the level of procedural error and have been described in more detail by Dahl and Bergeson (2009). Estimated procedural error ranged from 3 to 5 percent of the true values when all quality assurance measures had been completed. This error rate has remained steady since 2000.

Limitations

The identification and delineation of wetland habitats through image analysis forms the foundation for deriving the wetland status and trends data results reported here. Because of the limitations of aerial imagery as the primary data source to detect some wetlands, certain wetland types were excluded from this monitoring effort. These limitations included the inability to detect small wetland areas (see Sampling Design Section); inability to accurately detect or monitor certain types of wetlands such as seagrasses that may require hyperspectral or other specialized imagery or analysis techniques (Dierssen *et al.* 2003; Peneva *et al.* 2008), submerged aquatic vegetation, or submerged reefs (Dahl 2005); and inability to consistently identify certain forested wetlands either because of their small size, canopy closure, or lack of visible hydrology.

Figure 15. Earthen berms divide a farm field used in rotation with other crops for commercial rice production, Arkansas, 2010.

Other habitats intentionally excluded from data summary results in this study include:

Commercial Rice—Throughout the southeastern United States and in California, rice (*Oryza sativa*) is planted on drained hydric soils and on upland soils. When rice was being grown, the land was flooded and the area functioned as wetland. In years when rice was not grown, the same fields were used to grow other crops (e.g., corn, soybeans or cotton) as shown in Figure 15. Commercial rice lands were identified primarily in California, Arkansas, Louisiana, Mississippi and Texas. These cultivated rice fields were not able to support hydrophytic vegetation in the absence of artificial pumps. Consequently, these lands were not included in the base wetland acreage estimates.

Attribution of Wetland Losses

The process of identifying or attributing cause for wetland losses or gains has been investigated by both the Fish and Wildlife Service and Natural Resources Conservation Service (NRCS). In past studies, specialists from both agencies made a concerted effort to develop a uniform approach to attribute wetland losses and gains as to their causes (Dahl 2000). Interagency field evaluations were conducted to test these definitions on the wetland status and trends plot data. This was done by conducting field visits where interagency field teams evaluated a number of sites with different wetland types and changes in a variety of geographical locations. Field evaluations compared land use descriptors, wetland classification, and attribution of the losses or

gains observed. Ultimately, this process resulted in no disagreement among agency representatives with how wetland losses or gains were attributed as to cause. These descriptors have been used in subsequent reporting on wetland status and trends (Dahl 2000; 2006). The Fish and Wildlife Service and NRCS continue to coordinate on issues related to wetland change and attribution of those changes.

The USDA's Natural Resource Inventory (NRI) categorization of wetlands is slightly different than that used by the Fish and Wildlife Service's Wetlands Status and Trends study. The NRI and the Fish and Wildlife Service have different legislative mandates; sampling methodology, inventory protocols, data handling, and analysis routines have evolved independently, even though both survey programs use the hierarchical Cowardin *et al.* (1979) wetland classification system. Recent collaborative efforts have resulted in enhancements for both programs, but wetlands data collected by the two agencies are currently neither comparable nor interchangeable.

The categories used to determine the causes of wetland losses and gains are described below. Draining, filling or otherwise altering a wetland to conform to these land use descriptions constituted a loss in wetland area. Wetlands reestablished or created from these land use(s) constituted a gain in wetland area.

Agriculture

The definition of agriculture followed Anderson *et al.* (1976) and included land used primarily for production of food and fiber. Agricultural

activity was shown by distinctive geometric field and road patterns on the landscape and/or by tracks produced by livestock or mechanized equipment. Agricultural land uses included horticultural crops, row and close grown crops, hayland, pastureland, native pastures and range land and farm infrastructures. Examples of agricultural activities in each land use include:

Horticultural crops consisted of orchard fruits (limes, grapefruit, oranges, other citrus, apples, peaches, and like species). Also included were nuts such as almonds, pecans and walnuts; vineyards including grapes and hops; bush-fruit such as blueberries; berries such as strawberries or raspberries; and commercial flower and fern growing operations.

Row and Close Grown Crops included field corn, sugar cane, sweet corn, sorghum, soybeans, cotton, peanuts, tobacco, sugar beets, potatoes, and truck crops such as melons, beets, cauliflower, pumpkins, tomatoes, sunflower and watermelon. Close grown crops also included wheat, oats, barley, sod, ryegrass, and similar graminoids.

Hayland and pastureland included grass, legumes, summer fallow and grazed native grassland.

Other farmland included farmsteads and ranch headquarters, commercial feedlots, greenhouses, hog facilities, nurseries and poultry facilities.

Forested Plantations (Silviculture)

Forested plantations were uplands that consisted of planted and managed forests including planted pines, Christmas tree farms, clear cuts, and other managed forest stands. These were identified by the following remote sensing indicators: (1) trees planted in rows or blocks; (2) forested blocks growing with uniform crown heights; or (3) logging activity and use patterns (Figure 16).

Rural Development

Rural developments occurred in rural and suburban settings outside distinct cities and towns. This type of land use was disjunctive areas of development not within a well defined urbanized outgrowth or corridor. This classification shares only some of spatial characteristics of sprawl as found in the literature and summarized by Hasse (2007). Rural development was not based on number of dwelling units but may have included isolated infrastructure or development characterized by non-intensive land use and sparse building density. Scattered suburban communities located outside of major urban centers, described as "sprawl" (Wolman *et al.* 2005) also were included in this category as were some industrial and commercial complexes; isolated transportation, power, and communication facilities; strip mines; quarries; and recreational areas.

Urban Development

Urban land consisted of areas of intensive use in which much of the land was covered by structures (high building density). Urbanized areas were cities and towns that provided goods and services through a central business district. Services such as banking, medical and legal office buildings, supermarkets and department stores made up the business center of a city. Commercial strip developments along main transportation routes, shopping centers, dense residential areas, industrial and commercial complexes, transportation, power and communication facilities, city parks, ball fields and golf courses were included in the urban category.

Other Land Uses

Other Land Use was composed of uplands not characterized by the previous categories. Typically these lands included native prairie, unmanaged or non-patterned upland forests, conservation lands, scrub lands, and barren land.

Lands in transition between different uses also were in this category. These were lands in transition from one land use to another and generally occurred in large acreage blocks of 40 acres (16 ha) or more. They were characterized by the lack of any remote sensor information that would enable the interpreter to reliably predict future use. The transitional phase occurred when wetlands were drained, ditched, filled or when the vegetation had been removed and the area was temporarily bare.

Figure 16. Planted pine forest as an example of upland forested plantation, South Carolina, 2010. (Photograph by M. Bergeson, USFWS.)

Results

This study examined the status and recent trends of wetlands to monitor the changes in aerial extent from 2004 to 2009. Updated data on wetland area by type(s) and change information have been provided as well as new information derived from enhancing the study to include the estuarine wetlands along the Pacific coast of Washington, Oregon, and California. Because portions of the Pacific coastal region had not been sampled in previous wetland status and trends studies, there has been an adjustment to the total wetland area estimate for the conterminous United States. There also has been a statistical adjustment to the estimate of total wetland area for the United States[12].

The data presented here do not provide qualitative assessment nor do they address functional condition of the Nation's wetlands beyond changes in extent by type.

Status of the Nation's Wetlands

There were an estimated 110.1 million acres (44.6 million ha) of wetlands in the conterminous United States in 2009[13] (the coefficient of variation of the national estimate

was 2.7 percent). The percent of surface area and distribution by major wetland type had not changed since the previous era as wetlands composed 5.5 percent of the surface area of the conterminous U.S. An estimated 95 percent of all wetlands were freshwater and 5 percent were in the marine or estuarine (saltwater) systems. With the exception of minor statistical adjustments to the area estimates, the overall percentage of wetland area and representation by saltwater and freshwater components remained unchanged. In 2009, there were an estimated 104.3 million acres (42.2 million ha) of freshwater wetland and 5.8 million acres (2.4 million ha) of intertidal (saltwater) wetlands in the conterminous United States. Data for the 2004 to 2009 study period are presented in a change matrix and shown in Appendix D. The distribution of wetlands by type, estimated area and change has been summarized and presented in Table 2.

Within the marine and estuarine systems, estuarine emergent (salt marsh) made up an estimated 66.7 percent of all estuarine and marine intertidal wetland area (Figure 17). The mean size of salt marsh included in the sample was 34.6 acres (14.0 ha). Estuarine shrub wetlands made up an estimated 11.8 percent of the total intertidal wetland area in 2009. The mean size of estuarine shrub wetland sampled was 15.8 acres (6.4 ha). Non-vegetated intertidal wetlands represented 21.5 percent of all intertidal wetland area with a mean size of 11.8 acres (4.8 ha).

---

[12] The current estimate reflects a 2.0 percent adjustment to the national wetland acreage base. This was within the 2.7 percent coefficient of variation associated with the statistical estimate.

[13] This estimate has been revised to reflect 2010 wetland status as well as the addition of wetland area in the coastal zone of the Pacific coast for WA, OR, and CA as described in the Sample Design section of this report.

Table 2. Summary of study findings. Change in wetland area for selected wetland and deepwater categories, 2004 to 2009. The coefficient of variation (CV) for each entry (expressed as a percentage) is given in parentheses.

Wetland/Deepwater Category	Area, In Thousands of Acres			
	Estimated Area, 2004	Estimated Area, 2009	Change, 2004–2009	Change, (In Percent)
Marine Intertidal	219.2 (15.2)	227.8 (14.8)	8.5 (48.4)	3.9%
Estuarine Intertidal Non-Vegetated	999.4 (13.5)	1,017.7 (13.3)	18.3 (48.2)	1.8%
Estuarine Intertidal Vegetated [1]	4,650.7 (4.4)	4,539.7 (4.4)	-110.9 (16.6)	-2.4%
All Intertidal Wetlands	5,869.3 (4.6)	5,785.2 (4.6)	-84.1 (20.2)	-1.4%
Freshwater Ponds	6,502.1 (4.6)	6,709.3 (4.5)	207.2 (29.6)	3.2%
Freshwater Vegetated [2]	97,750.6 (2.9)	97,565.3 (2.9)	-185.3 (*)	-0.2%
Freshwater Emergent	27,162.7 (7.7)	27,430.5 (7.6)	267.8 (85.8)	1.0%
Freshwater Shrub	18,331.4 (4.2)	18,511.5 (4.2)	180.1 (*)	1.0%
Freshwater Forested	52,256.5 (2.7)	51,623.3 (2.7)	-633.1 (30.7)	-1.2%
All Freshwater Wetlands	104,252.7 (2.8)	104,274.6 (2.8)	21.9 (*)	0.0%
All Wetlands	110,122.1 (2.7)	110,059.8 (2.7)	-62.3 (*)	-0.1%
Lacustrine [3]	16,786.0 (10.1)	16,859.6 (10.1)	73.6 (60.0)	0.4%
Riverine	7,517.9 (8.7)	7,510.5 (8.7)	-7.4 (*)	-0.1%
Estuarine Subtidal	18,695.4 (2.5)	18,776.5 (2.5)	81.1 (25.4)	0.4%
All Deepwater Habitats	42,999.4 (4.3)	43,146.6 (4.3)	147.2 (33.8)	0.3%
All Wetlands and Deepwater Habitats	153,121.4 (2.4)	153,206.4 (2.4)	85.0 (*)	0.1%

* Statistically unreliable.

[1]Includes the categories: Estuarine Intertidal Emergent and Estuarine Intertidal Forested/Shrub.

[2]Includes the categories: Palustrine Emergent, Palustrine Shrub, and Palustrine Forested.

[3]Does not include the open-water area of the Great Lakes.

Percent coefficient of variation was expressed as (standard deviation/mean) × 100.

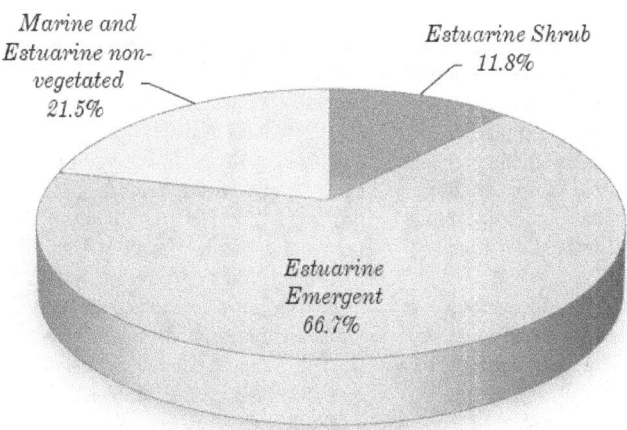

Figure 17. Status of estuarine wetland area by type, 2009.

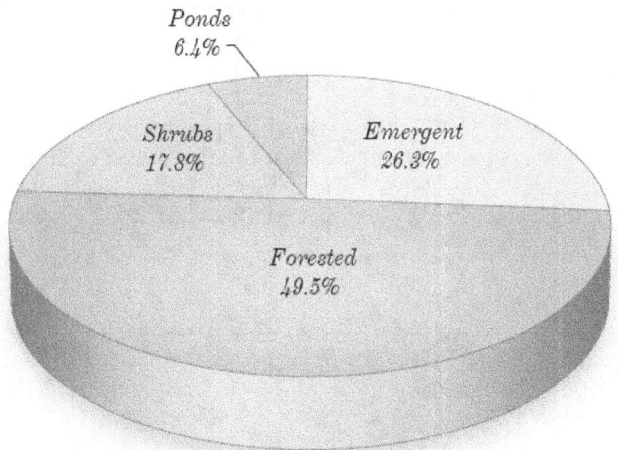

Figure 18. Status of freshwater wetland area by type, 2009.

Among the freshwater types, forested wetlands made up the single largest category (49.5 percent). Forested wetland area represented less than 50 percent of the total wetland acreage in the conterminous United States for the first time. The mean size of forested wetland was 20.3 acres (8.2 ha). Freshwater emergent wetland made up an estimated 26.3 percent of the total freshwater wetland area, shrub wetlands 17.8 percent and freshwater ponds 6.4 percent (Figure 18). The mean size of freshwater emergent, shrub and open water pond wetlands sampled in this study was 6.1 acres (2.5 ha), 7.6 acres (3.1 ha), and 1.3 acres (0.5 ha) respectively.

Wetlands were found in all 48 States and in every physiographic region of the country as part of this study. Spatial associations with land use types varied. Of the freshwater wetland population contained in the national sample, ponds were the most prevalent wetland type found in urban areas, whereas freshwater emergent wetlands were the least common type. On agricultural lands, there was a fairly even distribution of wetland types with forested, emergent and ponds represented. Land predominantly in silviculture had the highest percentage of forested and shrub wetland. Rural areas exhibiting growth had a mix of all freshwater wetland types, as they represented the interface of new development activities.

National Trends, 2004 to 2009

The difference in the national estimates of wetland acreage between 2004 and 2009 was not statistically significant. Wetland area declined by an estimated 62,300 acres (25,200 ha) between 2004 and 2009. This equated to an average annual loss of 13,800 acres (5,590 ha) during the 4.5 year time interval of this study (Figure 19) [14] as there were notable losses that occurred to intertidal estuarine emergent wetlands (salt marsh) and freshwater forested wetlands.

Collectively, marine and estuarine intertidal wetlands declined by an estimated 84,100 acres (34,050 ha). The loss rate of intertidal emergent wetland increased to three times the previous loss rate between 1998 and 2004. The majority of these losses

(83 percent) were to deepwater bay bottoms or open ocean. There were area gains in marine intertidal wetlands (beaches/shores) and estuarine non-vegetated wetlands including near shore shoals and sand bars. Over the period of this study, non-vegetated intertidal wetlands increased in area by an estimated 2.2 percent.

Freshwater vegetated wetlands continued to decline albeit at a reduced rate. The annual rate of loss for freshwater vegetated wetlands had been reduced by roughly 50 percent since 2004 (Figure 20). Declines in freshwater forested wetland area (633,100 acres or 256,300 ha) negated area gains in freshwater emergent and shrub categories. Forested wetlands sustained their largest losses since the 1974 to 1985 time period. An estimated 392,600 acres (158,950 ha) of forested wetland area was lost to upland land use types or deepwater between 2004 and 2009.

Gains in freshwater ponds offset losses of vegetated wetland area [15] although the 3.2 percent increase in pond area was four times less than reported in prior studies. The distribution of freshwater ponds by descriptive categories is shown in Figure 21 [16]. Farm ponds and ponds in urban (developed) areas increased, whereas ponds described as having natural characteristics and aquaculture ponds declined during the same time period. The overall estimated net gain in all freshwater wetland area (vegetated and non-vegetated types) between 2004 and 2009 was 21,900 acres (8,870 ha). This estimate had declined substantially from a net increase in freshwater wetland of 220,200 acres (89,140 ha) reported for the period between 1998 and 2004.

The estimated area of lacustrine and riverine deepwater habitats [17] increased slightly (<0.3 percent) between 2004 and 2009.

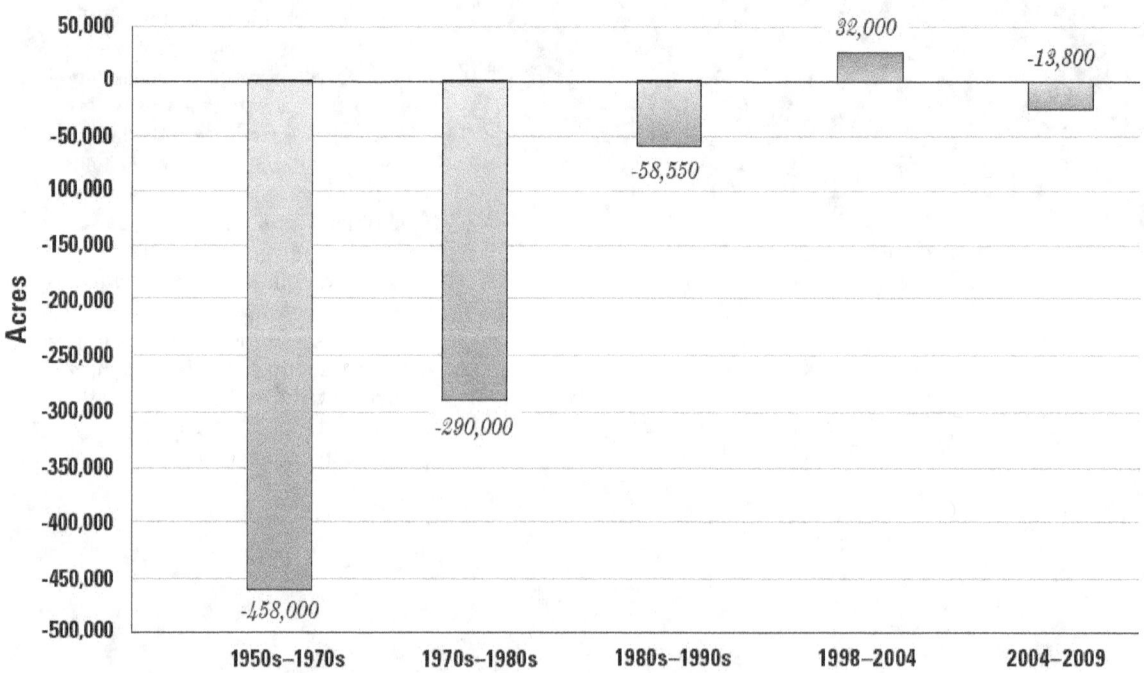

Figure 19. Average annual net loss and gain estimates for the conterminous United States, 1954 to 2009. Estimates of error are not graphically represented. Sources: Frayer et al. 1983; Dahl and Johnson 1991; Dahl 2000; 2006; and this study.

---

[14] There are statistical uncertainties associated with this estimate.

[15] This report did not draw any conclusions regarding trends in quality or condition of the any wetland type.

[16] Ponds were open-water bodies (freshwater) less than 20 acres (8.1 ha).

[17] Because of the sample design, these estimates do not represent total area of all freshwater lakes and rivers.

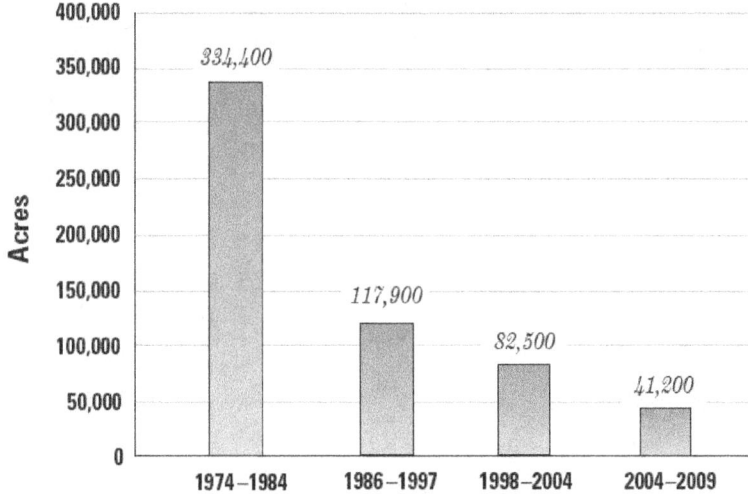

Figure 20. Estimated average annual loss of vegetated freshwater wetland area,[15] 1974 to 2009. Sources: Dahl and Johnson 1991; Dahl 2000; 2006; and this study.

[15] Includes palustrine forested, palustrine shrub and palustrine emergent wetlands.

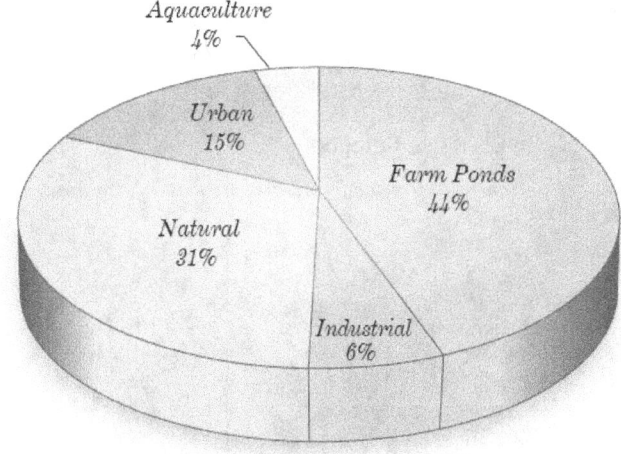

Figure 21. Percent occurrence of freshwater pond types, 2009.

Attribution of Wetland Gain and Loss, 2004 to 2009

Figure 22 illustrates the net gains and losses of wetlands that occurred between 2004 and 2009 relative to the various land use categories.

In the saltwater systems, there has been a trend toward an increase in non-vegetated tidal wetland as salt marsh areas have diminished. In combination, intertidal marine shorelines as well as estuarine flats, bars, and shoals increased in area and made up 21.5 percent of all intertidal wetlands in 2009.

This increase in tidal non-vegetated area came primarily from former salt marsh wetlands as estuarine emergent area declined by an estimated 111,500 acres (45,140 ha) or 2.8 percent between 2004 and 2009. One percent of the losses of salt marsh habitats were the result of conversion to upland land use. Eighty-three percent of the estuarine emergent losses were attributed to saltwater intrusion or other forms of inundation and the vast majority (99 percent) of all estuarine emergent losses were affected by open ocean generated processes (i.e., saltwater inundation, coastal storms, etc.). There was very little gain in estuarine vegetated wetland (either shrubs or emergent) as a result of reestablishment or creation during the time covered by this study.

Between 2004 and 2009, 489,600 acres (198,130 ha) of former upland were re-classified as wetland. These increases were attributed to wetland reestablishment and creation on agricultural lands and other uplands with undetermined land use (i.e., undeveloped land, lands in conservation programs or left idle). Further explanation of "other" uplands with undetermined land use has been provided in the inset (page 43). When these wetland gains were balanced with losses, freshwater wetlands realized a net increase of an estimated 21,900 acres (8,870 ha).

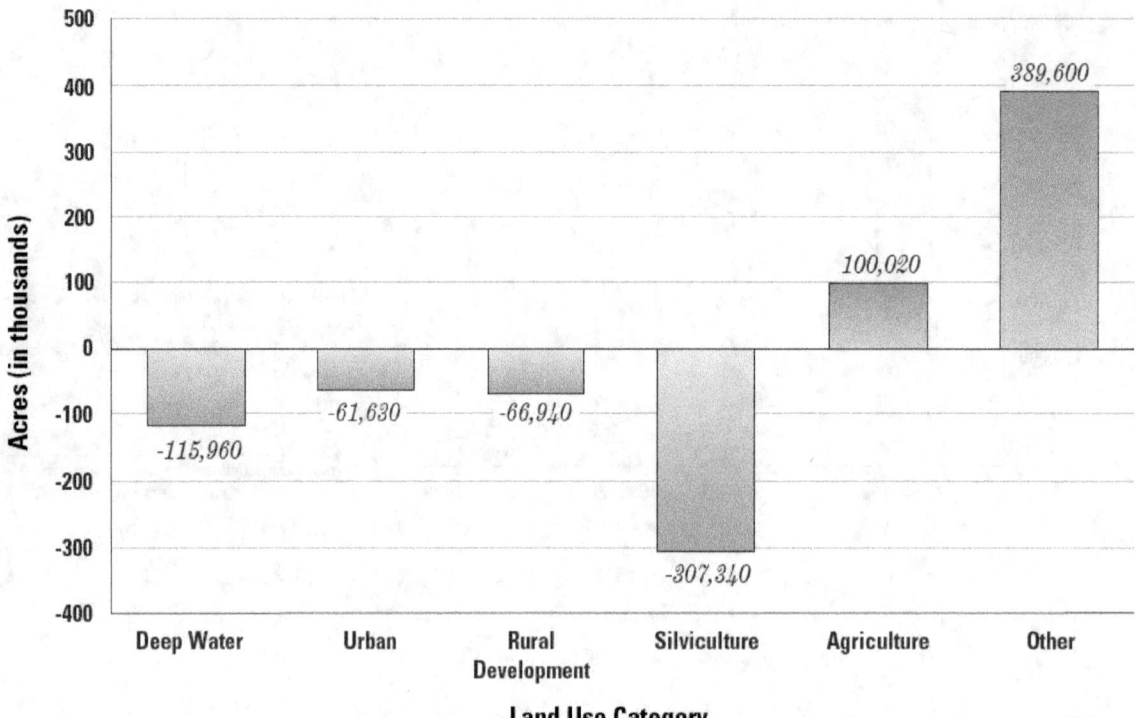

Figure 22. Estimated net gains and losses of wetland acres (saltwater and freshwater) attributed to the various upland land use categories and deepwater, 2004 to 2009.

Freshwater wetland losses were primarily attributed to urban and rural development and silviculture operations. Urban and rural development combined accounted for 23 percent of the wetland losses and were estimated to have been 128,570 acres (52,050 ha). This was an 8.0 percent decline in wetland area lost and attributed to urban or rural development as compared to the period between 1998 and 2004. Wetland losses to silviculture increased considerably since 2004. Silviculture accounted for 56 percent of all wetland losses from 2004 to 2009.

All freshwater wetland types increased in area with the exception of forested wetlands. Forested wetlands declined by 1.2 percent in area (633,100 acres or 256,200 ha). Attribution of the loss of freshwater forested wetland to uplands and deepwater from 2004 to 2009 is shown in Figure 23.

Freshwater ponds increased in area by 3.2 percent. An estimated 207,200 acres (83,890 ha) of freshwater ponds were created between 2004 and 2009. These wetlands ameliorated some of the

losses in area of other freshwater wetland types, but the functional characteristic of these water bodies continues to be debated.

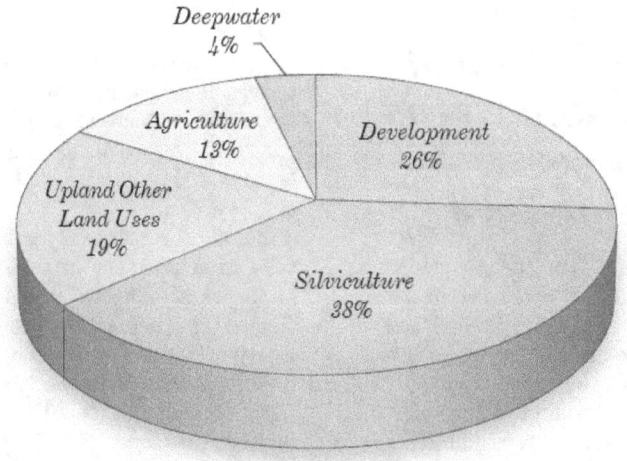

Figure 23. Loss of freshwater forested wetland as attributed to upland and deepwater categories, 2004 to 2009.

Wetland Gains and Loss Examples on "Other" Lands (Undetermined Land Use)

This study found that an estimated 389,600 acres (157,730 ha) net increase in wetland came from uplands classified as "other" lands or lands with undetermined land use. What are these "other" lands?

Other lands have included areas such as native prairie, unmanaged or non-patterned upland forests, scrub lands, barren and abandoned land, lands enrolled in set-aside programs, conservation easement or other lands designated as wildlife management areas. Lands in transition also may fit into this category when land has been cleared but not yet developed to the point of a distinguishable land use (i.e., silviculture or agriculture) as seen in Figure 24.

Wetland changes attributed to "other" lands have become more prominent. This has been due to the success of conservation programs that have developed streamside buffers, soil conservation measures, crop retirement programs, easements and land set-aside programs. As some of these areas have been enlisted into conservation programs, wetlands have been reestablished either by design or through natural processes (Figure 25). Natural changes on "other" lands such as buffers along stream corridors or in riparian areas were not uncommon. Riparian dynamics have the ability to create and destroy wetlands along stream corridors or in floodplains (Kudray and Schemm 2008).

Figure 24. Wetland losses attributed to "other" land use indicated the land may be in transition from one land use to another and the final land use type can not be determined. This example of a wetland area in the process of being drained and filled provided no indication of the final land characterization (South Carolina, 2010, photograph by M. Bergeson, USFWS).

Figure 25. This temporarily flooded wetland has reestablished naturally on lands that were part of an agricultural program set-aside. The surrounding upland was no longer in active agriculture and was classified as "other" upland (Minnesota, 2009).

Crystal River, FL.
Photograph courtesy of USFWS

Discussion and Analysis

This study, as a long-term monitoring effort, has helped document the historical trends in wetland gains and losses and traced policy and land use practices that have had consequences for these resources. At the time the study was originated (1970s), the average annual wetland loss rate was 458,000 acres (185,400 ha). During the period between the mid-1970s to mid-1980s, the loss rate had declined to 290,000 acres (117,400 ha) annually. In 1998, the wetland loss rate was about 59,000 acres (23,900 ha) annually and in 2005 wetland area gains had exceeded losses by an estimated 32,000 acres (13,000 ha) per year.

Wetland losses increased between 2004 and 2009 reversing this long-standing trend in wetland loss reduction. The reasons for this were complex and subject to many factors including economic conditions (such as crop prices or property values), land use trends, changes to wetland regulation and enforcement measures and possible climatic changes.

Data indicate that the rate of wetland reestablishment or creation between 2004 and 2009 increased by 17 percent from the previous study period (1998 and 2004). Yet, the overall estimated net gain in all freshwater wetland area (vegetated and non-vegetated types) between 2004 and 2009 was 21,900 acres

(8,870 ha), a substantially lower net increase than the 220,200 acres (89,140 ha) reported for the period between 1998 and 2004. A comparable analysis of the wetland loss rate showed an increase of 140 percent from 2004 to 2009 from the previous era. As a consequence, national wetland losses have outdistanced gains.

Marine and Estuarine Wetlands

Table 3 shows the current status and change for the marine and estuarine intertidal (saltwater) wetlands between 2004 and 2009. Cowardin *et al.* (1979) defined "estuarine" and "marine" wetlands as saltwater systems. Marine and estuarine wetlands have been grouped into three types: estuarine intertidal emergent wetlands (salt and brackish water marshes), estuarine shrub wetlands (mangrove swamps and other salt-tolerant woody species), and estuarine and marine intertidal non-vegetated wetlands. This latter category included exposed coastal beaches subject to tidal flooding, as well as sand bars, tidal sand or mud flats, shoals, and sand spits. These tidal wetlands are subjected to a multitude of anthropogenic stressors originating from the landward side,

natural forces affecting change from the sea (Stedman and Dahl 2008), as well as increasing sea levels and climatic change. There is growing awareness of the threats posed by climate related changes on fresh and saltwater systems in coastal areas. Recently, the Army Corps of Engineers and NOAA published frameworks to guide how to consider the impacts of factors such as sea level rise in coastal wetlands (USEPA 2010a).

Saltwater intertidal wetlands are dynamic areas of tremendous ecological, economic and social importance. The ecological value of tidal wetlands has been well documented by a number of researchers (Mitsch and Gosselink 2007; Costanza *et al.* 2008; Harrington 2008; USEPA 2008) as these wetlands provide crucial migratory habitat for the majority of shorebirds that breed in the United States (Withers 2002); support adult stocks of commercially harvested shrimp, blue crabs, oysters, and other species of fish and shellfish (Stedman and Hanson 2000); and provide protection from storms (Costanza *et al.* 2008). In the Pacific Northwest, coastal fishes and particularly anadromous species such as the salmonids, utilize coastal marshes as areas to transition from freshwater to open ocean environments (Adamus 2005; Simenstad *et al.* 2002).

Table 3. Status and changes to intertidal marine and estuarine wetlands, 2004 to 2009. The coefficient of variation (CV) for each entry (expressed as a percentage) is given in parentheses.

Wetland/Deepwater Category	Area, In Thousands of Acres				Area (as percent) of all Intertidal Wetlands, 2009
	Estimated Area, 2004	Estimated Area, 2009	Change, 2004–2009	Change, (In Percent)	
Marine Intertidal	219.2 (15.2)	227.8 (14.8)	8.5 (48.4)	3.9%	3.9%
Estuarine Intertidal Non-Vegetated	999.4 (13.5)	1,017.7 (13.3)	18.3 (48.2)	1.8%	17.6%
Marine and Estuarine Intertidal Non-Vegetated	1,218.6 (11.5)	1,245.5 (11.2)	26.8 (35.3)	2.2%	21.5%
Estuarine Emergent	3,971.4 (4.6)	3,859.8 (4.7)	-111.5 (16.6)	-2.8%	66.7%
Estuarine Forested/Shrub	679.3 (12.4)	679.9 (12.4)	0.6 (*)	0.1%	11.8%
Estuarine Intertidal Vegetated [1]	4,607.7 (4.4)	4,539.7 (4.4)	-110.9 (16.6)	-2.4%	78.5%
Changes in Coastal Deepwater area, 2004–2009					
All Estuarine and Marine Intertidal	5,869.3 (4.6)	5,785.2 (4.6)	-84.1 (20.2)	-1.4%	–

* *Statistically unreliable.*

[1] *Includes the categories: Estuarine Intertidal Emergent and Estuarine Intertidal Forested/Shrub. Percent coefficient of variation was expressed as (standard deviation/mean) × 100.*

Trends in Estuarine Emergent (Salt Marsh) Wetland

The largest acreage change in the saltwater system was an estimated loss of more than 111,500 acres (45,140 ha) of estuarine emergent wetland (salt marsh as shown in Figure 26). This rate of loss was three times greater than estuarine emergent losses from 1998 to 2004 and continued a long-term trend in the decline of estuarine emergent wetland area. In this study, there were very few (< 1 percent) estuarine emergent losses attributed to discrete anthropogenic actions[19] that fill or otherwise convert salt marsh areas to uplands.

[19] Land subsidence and sea level rise may be attributed to human actions but could not be traced to a specific event or geospatial change such as filling, draining, or otherwise mechanically altering wetland area.

Figure 26. Estuarine salt marsh wetland, Florida, 2010.

This suggests that marine and estuarine vegetated wetlands (tidal salt marsh and shrubs) have been afforded protection by various State and Federal coastal regulatory measures including Federal protection under the Section 404 of the Clean Water Act as waters of the United States (Dahl 2000). These wetlands, however, have been susceptible to oceanic influences including sea level rise and storm events. An estimated 99 percent of the losses of estuarine emergent wetlands between 2004 and 2009 were attributed to effects from coastal storms, land subsidence, sea level rise, or other ocean processes (Figure 27) and the vast majority of these losses were in the northern Gulf of Mexico along the coastline of Louisiana and Texas.

Factors responsible for the loss of estuarine emergent wetland in the northern Gulf included land subsidence (sinking of the land), compaction of sediments and extraction of subsurface fluids, such as oil, gas, and water. In portions of coastal Louisiana and Texas, oil, gas, and groundwater extractions have been recognized as factors that contributed to subsidence and relative sea level rise (Galloway *et al.* 1999; Morton *et al.* 2003; Dokka 2006; Lavoie 2009). Throughout the northern Gulf coastal region, marine and estuarine wetlands have been adversely impacted by the cumulative effects of energy development (Figure 28), coastal storms and development in the upper portions of the watershed.

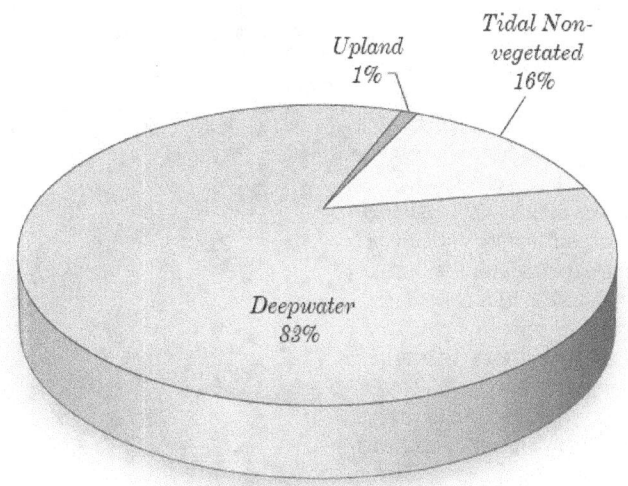

Figure 27. The attribution of estuarine emergent (salt marsh) losses between 2004 and 2009. An estimated 99 percent of these losses were attributed to deepwater and tidal non-vegetated areas and were the result of coastal storms or ocean derived processes.

Figure 28. Oil and gas field development located in estuarine (salt-marsh) wetlands of southern Louisiana. Such modifications have increased the vulnerability of these wetlands to climate related change (Twilley 2007) and the cumulative impacts have contributed to relative sea level rise, marsh fragmentation, and subsidence.

The construction of levees and canals, such as the hundreds of miles of Mississippi River levees constructed to control flooding, also weaken the sustainability of the landscape and have contributed to coastal wetlands loss (GAO 2007). These actions have reduced freshwater and sediment that has been crucial to maintain estuarine wetland elevation as a mechanism to overcome rising sea levels. In these areas and elsewhere, wetlands have been vulnerable to salt water intrusion and marsh disintegration as development has interfered with natural hydrological processes that transport sediment and freshwater necessary to sustain the structure, function, and extent of wetland ecosystems (Kling and Sanchirico 2009). The interconnection between fresh and saltwater systems has become more apparent as impacts to freshwater wetlands have compounded the effects of sea level rise and the ability of wetlands in coastal watersheds to adapt.

Since the mid-1980s, there has been recognition that the majority of losses to these tidal wetlands have resulted from coastal erosion and inundation by salt water. This situation has been exacerbated by a series of hurricanes in the Gulf of Mexico that damaged property and natural resources in proximity to coastal areas. Attempts to re-nourish tidal wetlands have been implemented following several hurricane events from 2005 to 2008 (Figure 29). There also has been considerable work in the northern Gulf of Mexico to armor near-shore areas that were damaged as a result of hurricanes or relative rise in sea level.

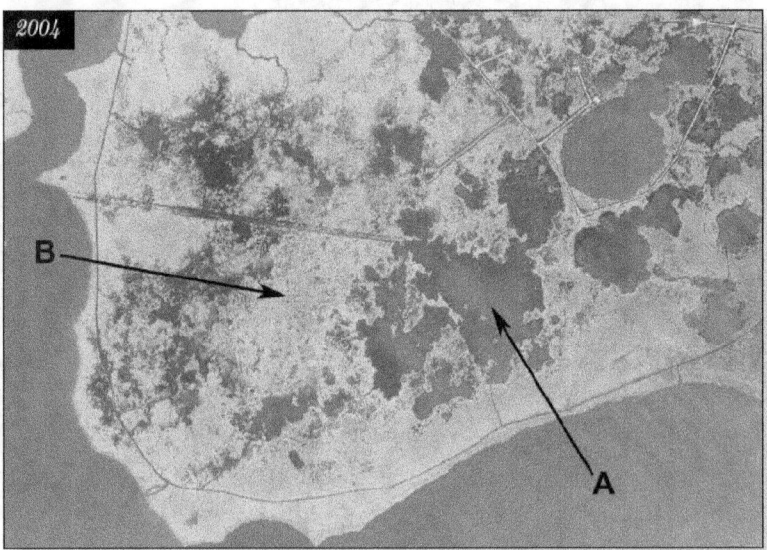

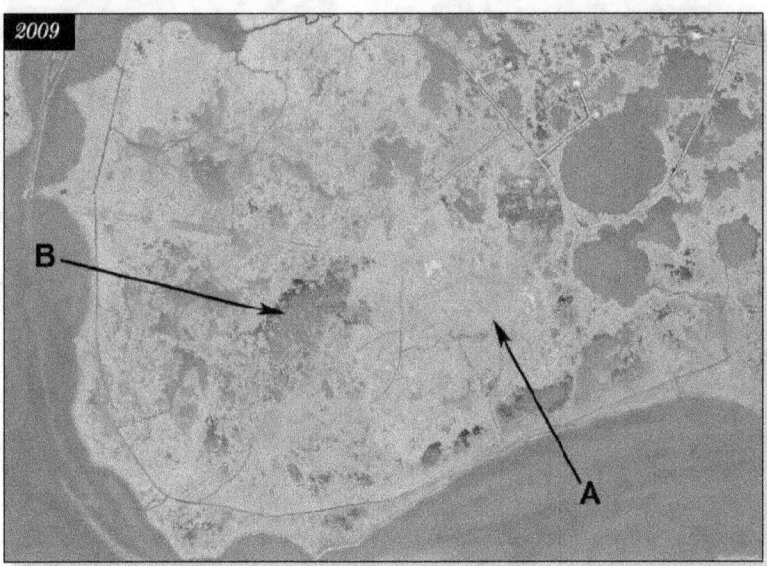

Figure 29. Comparison of aerial images from 2004 (top) and 2009 (bottom) showing areas of estuarine marsh along the northern Texas coast. At site A, the open water (dark blue) in this color infrared (CIR) image has been restored to emergent marsh seen as gray or brown in the true-color image in 2009. Wetland mitigation was completed in 2008 using approximately 500,000 cubic yards (381,680 cubic meters) of dredge material to restore 240 acres (97 ha) of open water to emergent marsh. Site B seen as emergent salt marsh (reddish color) in the 2004 CIR image, has been impacted by a series of tropical storms including Hurricane Rita (2005), Hurricane Humberto (2007) and Hurricane Ike (2008). The 2009 true-color image shows this wetland area has been physically scoured removing the marsh vegetation and inundated by high salinity sea water (olive-green color). Marsh losses also have been accentuated by regional drought conditions.

The data from this study provided little evidence of increased estuarine wetland area resulting from reestablishment. Wetland reestablishment (restoration) or creation has been more challenging in tidal systems and potentially more costly where land values fueled by development were high. Additionally, successful reestablishment of many tidal wetlands has hinged on consideration of physical processes including flow, circulation, and transport of nutrients, salinity and sediments (Sanders and Arega 2002). Because of the recent storm events along the Gulf coast, local, State and Federal agencies have renewed their emphasis on coastal wetland reestablishment (Working Group for Post-Hurricane Planning for the Louisiana Coast, 2006; Twilley 2007; Day et al. 2008).

Under the auspices of the Coastal Wetlands Planning, Protection and Restoration Act (CWPPRA), Federal agencies and the State of Louisiana have designed and/or constructed 147 projects intended to restore and protect more than 120,000 acres of coastal wetlands (Government Accountability Office [GAO] 2007). Some of these projects included wetland and land protection efforts, salinity control and water diversion. Some projects have yet to be implemented and as a consequence, the results have not been recognized as wetland acreage gains. A review conducted by GAO indicated that of the 147 projects, 22 were demonstration projects and 17 projects had been delayed due to problems such as land rights, oyster leases, and uncertain benefits of the project design. Shoreline protection projects (building barriers from rock or plants, see Figure 30) and hydrologic restoration projects (returning areas to their natural drainage patterns) made up more than one-half of the 90 projects that were completed or under construction. An example of a large scale project designed to trap sediment and restore estuarine marsh is shown in Figure 31. The CWPPRA program also has faced several challenges, such as increasing project costs, limited capability to monitor project effectiveness, uncertain project performance, issues with private landowner rights, and damage from hurricanes and storms (GAO 2007). Additionally, the GAO found that many of these projects were expected to erode and subside over time as a result of naturally occurring hydrologic and geologic processes.

Figure 30. An example of shoreline protection measures along the coast of southeastern Louisiana. Rock outcrops have been systematically placed in shallow water parallel to the shoreline.

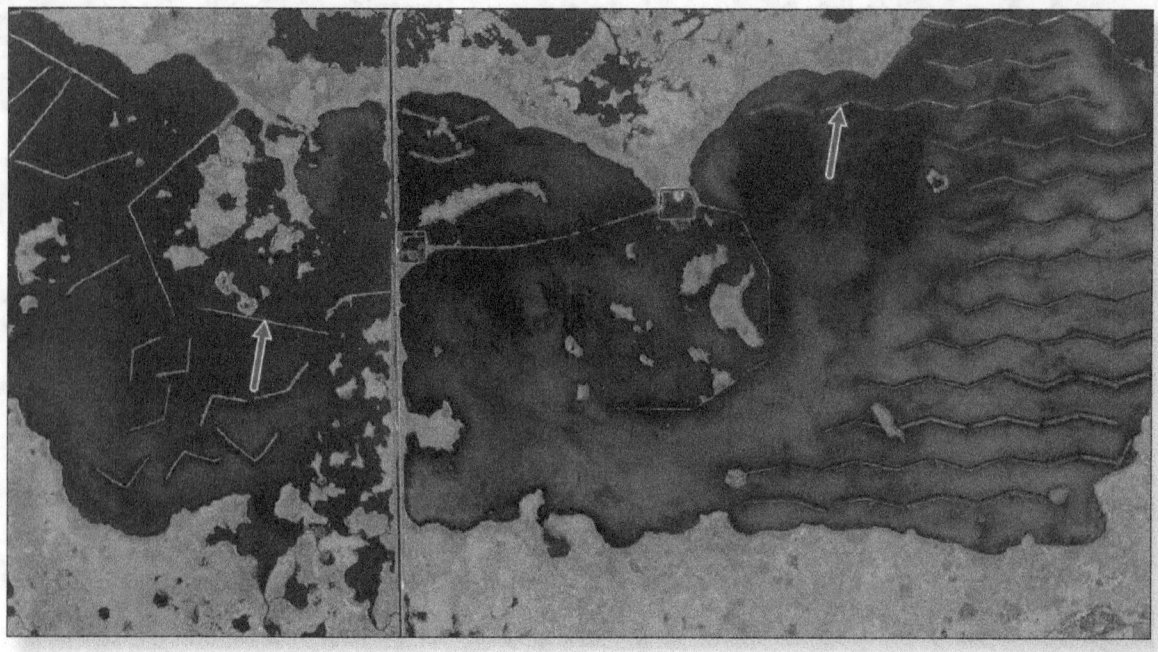

Figure 31. Man-made structures (identified by red arrows) in areas of former estuarine marsh in southern Louisiana. Projects such as this were designed to trap sediment and hopefully reestablish vegetation.

Estuarine Shrub Wetlands

Estuarine shrub wetlands were comprised of halophytic trees and shrubs growing in brackish or saline tidal waters. This category was dominated by species of mangroves (*Rhizophora mangle, Avicennia germinans,* and *Laguncularia racemosa*) but also may have included other salt tolerant woody species, such as buttonwood (*Conocarpus erectus*), saltbush (*Baccharis halimifolia*), bay cedar (*Suriana maritina*), and false willow (*Baccharis angustifolia*). Mangrove dominated wetlands (Figure 32) serve as valuable nurseries for a variety of recreationally and commercially important marine species (National Park Service 2010).

Overall, estuarine shrubs had a small net gain in area (0.1 percent) as losses to upland were outdistanced by gains. Area gains in estuarine shrubs came from both palustrine wetlands (1,789 acres or 724 ha), presumably from salt water inundation of low lying freshwater wetland[20]; and from agricultural lands and unspecified other uplands (2,314 acres or 937 ha collectively). There were an estimated 1,370 acres (555 ha) of estuarine shrub wetlands lost to upland between 2004 and 2009. Eighty-three percent of those losses were attributed to urbanization and related development. Human induced impacts to mangrove wetlands included proliferation of invasive species, cutting/removal, coastal development resulting in drainage, filling or changes to shoreline structure.

Long-term trends in area of estuarine shrub wetland has remained fairly constant since the 1980s despite long-term stressors including invasion by exotic species such as Brazilian pepper (*Schinus terebinthifolius*) and a high vulnerability to change due to natural causes such as coastal storms, drought, frost, fire, sea level changes and stress due to increased salinity. Climax stands of mangrove forest are uncommon in the conterminous United States as they survive within a very limited geographic range and have been vulnerable to physical damage from high winds that accompany coastal storms.

---

[20] Saltwater inundation of other woody species also was possible.

Figure 32. Mangrove shrub wetlands along the west coast of Florida.

Marine and Estuarine Non-Vegetated Wetlands

Non-vegetated coastal wetland habitats included tidal flats, shoals, sandbars, sandy beaches and small barrier islands. Study findings provided new information about the extent of tidal non-vegetated wetland along the Pacific coast of the conterminous United States. An estimated 40 percent of all non-vegetated tidal wetlands were found along the near-shore areas of the Pacific coast (Figure 33). Most of these non-vegetated tidal wetlands were located around Puget Sound, Willapa Bay and Grays Harbor in Washington; Tillamook Bay and Coos Bay in Oregon; and San Francisco Bay, California. The extent of these wetlands remained stable when compared to the same type of areas of the Atlantic and Gulf of Mexico. The Pacific coast of the conterminous United States experienced no change in the estimated area of tidal non-vegetated wetland between 2004 and 2009, and insignificant (<100 acres or 41 ha) change in estuarine vegetated wetland area.

In contrast, intertidal non-vegetated wetlands along the Atlantic and the Gulf of Mexico sustained considerable change. Over the time-span of this study the area of intertidal non-vegetated wetland increased by an estimated 2.2 percent (26,800 acres or 10,850 ha). All of these changes occurred along the south Atlantic and Gulf coastlines and were attributed to storm events that transported sediments, over-washed barrier islands, or scoured shorelines and other near-shore features along the coast. Intertidal non-vegetated wetlands (shores and flats) have

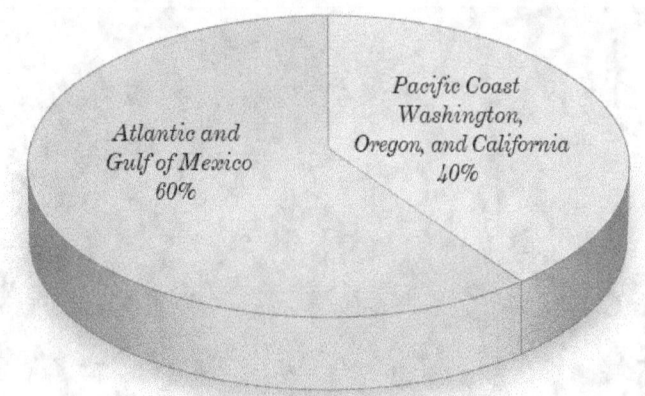

Figure 33. Estimated percent area of intertidal non-vegetated wetland along the Pacific coastline of Washington, Oregon, and California compared to the coastline of the Atlantic and Gulf of Mexico, 2009.

exhibited marked change and instability and, despite an increase in acreage, are most likely to sustain additional changes from ongoing and future coastal processes (Figure 34). Seaward events such as storms, tidal-surge causing erosion and deposition, saltwater intrusion and inundation have contributed to the modification of these coastal wetland types and extent (Steadman and Dahl 2008).

The effects on non-vegetated wetland types has often been overshadowed by losses to vegetated wetland areas, but these wetlands provide crucial habitats for a variety of coastal bird species, including pelicans, cormorants, gulls, terns, and roughly 50 species of sandpipers, plovers, and their allies known as shorebirds. (Harrington and Corven [no date]) have described shorebird guilds, enumerating species and habitat types.) Some of these bird

populations are at risk because of their dependence on narrow ribbons of marine and estuarine tidal habitats that are subjected to rapid and unpredictable changes resulting from coastal storms, habitat alteration by man, and other changes in marine ecosystems that can affect the availability of marine invertebrates (a food resource), water temperature, nutrients, and phytoplankton. Rising sea levels are expected to continue to inundate or fragment low-lying coastal areas including sandy beaches, barrier islands, and mudflats that support sea and shorebirds dependent on marine waters (North American Bird Conservation Initiative [NABCI] 2010) (Figure 35A and 35B).

Figure 34. The fishing pier on Dauphin Island, Alabama, no longer reaches the water line as coastal sediments have been deposited along this shore (2010).

Figures 35 A and 35B. Sea birds (A) including these Royal Terns and Black Skimmers rest and feed on intertidal habitats such as beaches and tidal flats (Photograph by J. Dahl). At lower tides, shorebirds (B) prefer foraging on invertebrates characteristic of sandy, intertidal habitats, such as sandbars or barrier beaches (Harrington 2008). Pictured are Short-billed Dowitcher (Limnodromus griseus) and Willet (Tringa semipalmata). (Photograph by A. Cruz, USFWS).

Most recently, tidal beaches, shoals, bars, and barrier islands along the northern Gulf of Mexico were exposed to the impacts from the *Deepwater Horizon* oil spill (Figure 36). Although data on any wetland losses resulting from that event are not included in these results[21], the incident served to highlight the ecological and economic importance of these marine and estuarine resources.

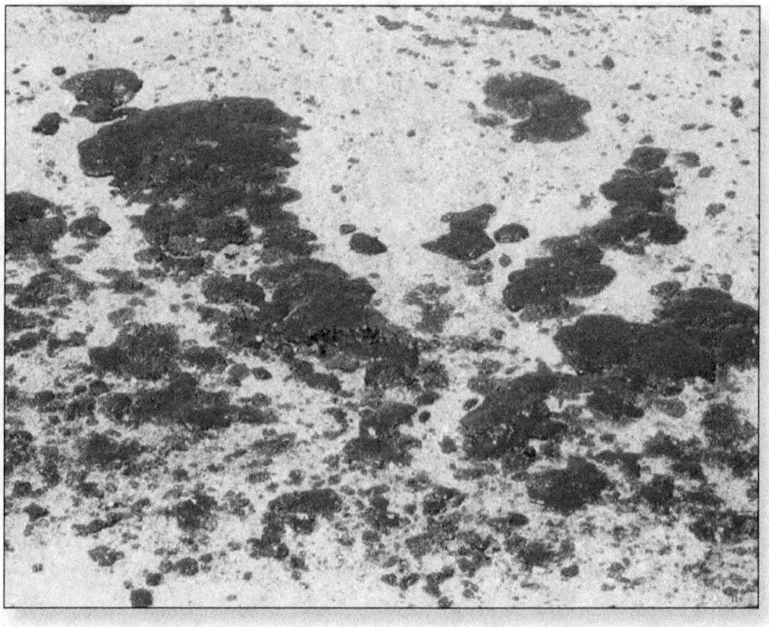

Figure 36. Beached oil from the Deepwater Horizon oil spill, 2010. (Photograph courtesy of Denise Rowell, Alabama Ecological Services Field Office, USFWS).

Changes in Sea Level and Coastal Processes Affecting Marine and Estuarine Wetlands

There is strong scientific consensus that climate change is accelerating sea level rise and affecting coastal regions, however, many researchers point to the uncertainties associated with predicting the response that increased sea level will have given other coastal processes and interactions (National Academy of Sciences 2008; Lavoie 2009). Sea level rise directly threatens coastal infrastructure through inundation, increased erosion, more frequent storm-surge flooding, and loss of habitat through drowned wetlands (NOAA Congressional Budget Hearing 2009). Coastal habitats will likely be increasingly stressed by climate change impacts that have resulted from sea level rise and coastal storms of increasing frequency and intensity (Field *et al.* 2007). The difficulty in linking sea level rise to coastal change stems from shoreline changes not solely the result of sea level rise

(Lavoie 2009). Natural and physical processes that act on the coast (e.g., storms, waves, currents, sand sources, sinks, relative sea level), as well as human actions that affect coastal processes in both the saltwater and freshwater systems, (e.g., development, dredging, dams, coastal engineering and modification), all have contributed to coastal changes.

In the conterminous United States, the Gulf of Mexico and mid-Atlantic coasts have experienced the highest rates of relative sea level rise and recent wetland loss (NABCI 2010). Stedman and Dahl (2008) found that in addition to the wetland losses already recognized, climate change models project additional wetland degradation in coastal areas as sea level continues to rise throughout this century. This trend has presented long-term challenges to managing and monitoring wetlands that abut the coast in coming decades.

---

[21] The period covered by this study was 2004 to 2009.

Inundation of coastal wetlands by rising sea levels threatens wetland plants particularly those not able to adjust to higher salinities or increased wave or tidal energy. For many of these systems to persist, a continued input of suspended sediment from inflowing streams and rivers is required for soil accretion (Poff *et al.* 2002). Migration or movement of coastal wetlands may offset some losses; however, this possibility is limited in areas with cliffs and steeper topography, such as areas on the Pacific Coast (Figure 37) and parts of the north Atlantic or, where shorelines are extensively developed (e.g., around Mobile Bay, Pensacola Bay, Tampa Bay, Biscayne Bay, portions of Chesapeake Bay, and San Francisco Bay). The construction of levees and flood protection infrastructure may put some wetlands at additional risk by restricting water flow, sediment, and nutrient inputs. Corbett *et al.* (2008) estimated that about 30 percent of the shoreline along the Neuse River Estuary in North Carolina had been modified with stabilization structures. Coastal development, urbanization, and infrastructure to support tourism throughout the coastal watersheds have an increased cumulative effect on the loss and modification of freshwater and estuarine wetland habitats. With continued growth and development, more shorelines have been cleared and stabilized (Figure 38), shallow waters dredged for navigation channels and marinas, wetlands filled and channelized, and land surfaces paved for buildings and parking lots (Riggs and Ames 2003).

Figure 37. Cliffs and rocky shorelines along California's Pacific coastline restrict any possible migration (retreat) of coastal wetlands as sea levels rise.

Figure 38. Shoreline armoring and stabilization along this beach in North Carolina was designed to protect coastal dunes and development.

Figure 39. Eroding shoreline along the Atlantic coast in Georgia.

Data from this study and others show that beach erosion due to sea level rise has increased along certain shorelines (Figure 39). This has constrained coastal plants to narrow stretches of beach and resulted in a breakdown of the succession processes that have been important for dune building, sediment binding, and reduction of erosion (Feagin *et al.* 2005) (Figure 40).

Rising sea levels and coastal storms are expected to contribute to the loss of beaches and barrier islands, particularly on the Atlantic Coast (Hanemann *et al.* 2003). Morton and Miller (2005) estimated that between 1970 and 2000, 39 percent of the 1,543 km of the Southeast Atlantic Coast that was surveyed had eroded, despite efforts to mitigate shoreline and barrier island loss through nourishment and reinforcement. The State of Florida has classified approximately 46 percent of the State's beaches as sustaining "critical erosion" (Florida Department of Environmental Protection 2008). Increased human activities have diminished major

sand sources, resulting in either the total loss or a more transitory nature of some beaches as they erode at increased rates (Riggs and Ames 2003). Modifications to some coastal features such as barrier islands include construction of barrier dune ridges, planting of stabilizing vegetation and urban development that can curtail or even eliminate the natural processes that help maintain these systems (Smith *et al.* 2008). Because of the position on the landscape, these wetlands are the first to interface with the coastal marine environment (Day *et al.* 2008) and bear the brunt of tides, wave action, and any increased inundation that cause erosion, movement and scouring of intertidal sediments. These stressors have resulted in changes to tidal non-vegetated wetlands corresponding to the location of coastal storms, erosion, translocation and re-deposition of sediments and have been reflected in the data reported here.

Intuitively, the locations most vulnerable to sea level rise have the lowest regional coastal slopes (Beavers 2002) and possess physiographic characteristics that make them susceptible to sea water intrusion, erosion or inundation. Tidal non-vegetated wetlands (beaches, sand bars, shoals, sand and mud flats and small barrier islands) have been especially susceptible to increases in sea level and other climatic changes, such as warming sea temperatures and increasing coastal storm frequency and intensity.

Mangroves and other forested ecosystems directly adjacent to saltwater coastlines also have been prone to change because of their narrow environmental requirements and geographic and climatic limitations along tidal fringe environments. Their susceptibility to physical–structural damage and the reduced ability of some shorelines to withstand coastal storms put these forested wetland communities at risk. More frequent or longer lasting droughts and reduced freshwater inflows may increase the incidence of extreme salt concentrations in coastal ecosystems, resulting in a decline of mangroves (Krauss *et al.* 2008) and other maritime woody species. Along portions of the west coast of Florida, saltwater intrusion has already replaced forested habitats with salt marsh or more salt tolerant species—a more subtle ecological shift than the drowning of coastal vegetation by rising sea levels associated with saltwater inundation (Williams *et al.* 1999). In the future, mangrove forests may be diminished in both stature and extent (Doyle 1997) as their extent, stability, and ecological integrity are threatened by increased wave action, coastal storm events, changes in water temperature, depth, and duration of tidal inundation.

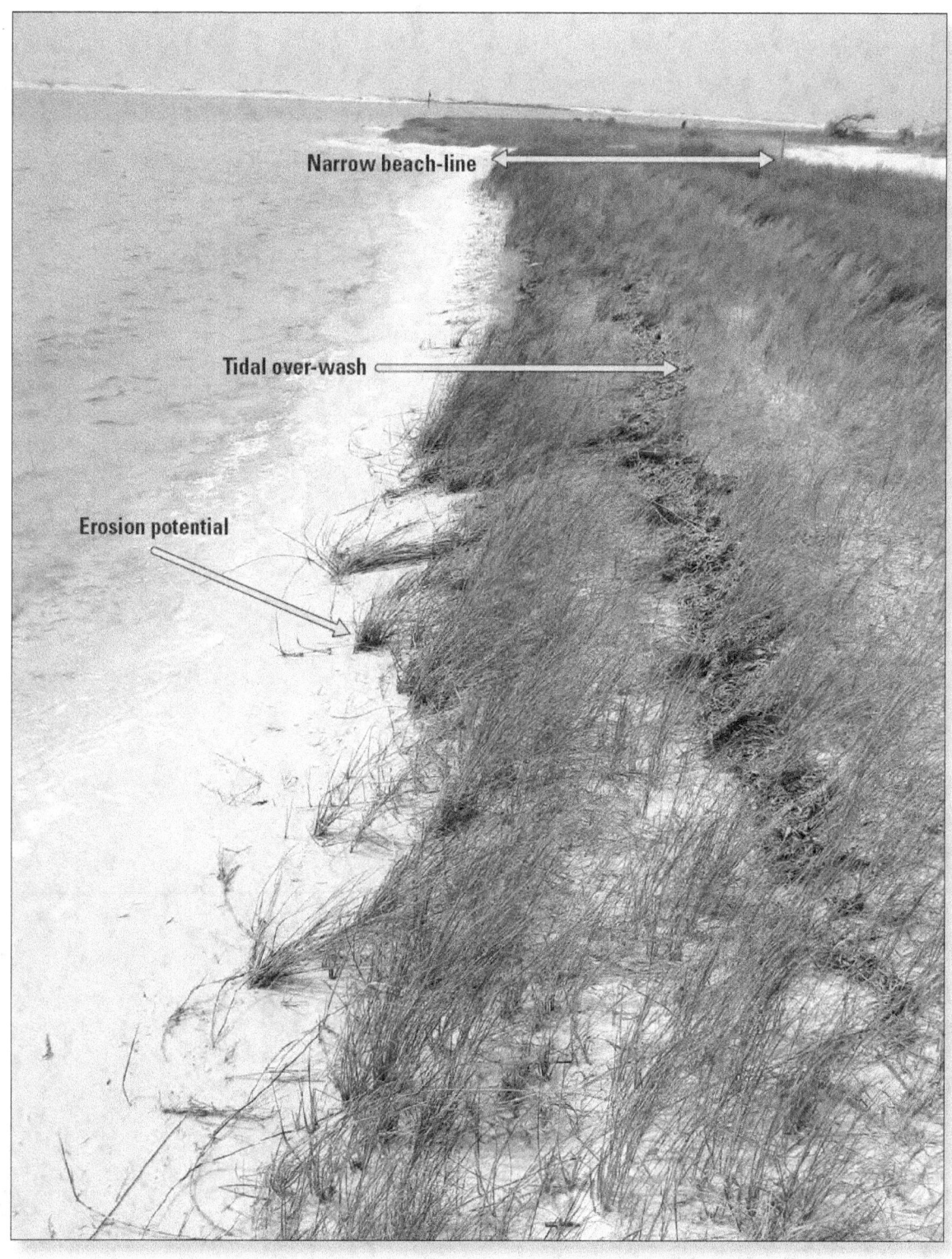

Narrow beach-line

Tidal over-wash

Erosion potential

Figure 40. Estuarine shoreline along the northwestern Florida coast illustrated the effects of erosion and confinement of coastal plants to a narrow beach-line. These areas have been susceptible to inundation and over wash (Photograph by M. Bergeson, USFWS).

Freshwater Wetlands

Freshwater wetlands were diverse, widely distributed and made up an estimated 95 percent of the total wetland area in the conterminous United States in 2009. They included small, isolated depressions as well as extensive forest-marsh complexes. Freshwater wetlands provide numerous ecological and socio-economic services (Mitsch and Gosselink 2007). The current status and change by wetland category for the freshwater (palustrine) wetlands is shown in Table 4.

Between 2004 and 2009, collectively, freshwater wetland types had an estimated net gain in area of 21,900 acres (8,900 ha). This slight increase was largely supported by the increased area in freshwater ponds. Freshwater vegetated wetlands declined by 0.2 percent in area over the same time period with losses of forested wetlands.

There were four principle types of freshwater wetlands described in this study: freshwater emergent marshes, freshwater shrubs, freshwater forested wetlands, and freshwater ponds. Trend information for each of these types is discussed below.

Table 4. Status and changes in freshwater wetland types between 2004 to 2009. The coefficient of variation (CV) for each entry (expressed as a percentage) is given in parentheses.

Wetland Category	Area, In Thousands of Acres				Area (as Percent of all Freshwater Wetlands, 2009
	Estimated Area, 2004	Estimated Area, 2009	Change, 2004–2009	Change, (In Percent)	
Freshwater Emergent	27,162.7 (7.7)	27,430.5 (7.6)	267.8 (85.8)	1.0%	26.3%
Freshwater Shrub	18,331.4 (4.2)	18,511.5 (4.2)	180.1 (*)	1.0%	17.8%
Freshwater Forested	52,256.5 (2.7	51,623.3 (2.7)	-633.1 (30.7)	-1.2%	49.5%
Freshwater Vegetated Wetlands	97,750.6 (2.9)	97,565.3 (2.9)	-185.3 (*)	-0.2%	93.6%
Aquaculture Ponds	380.7 (27.6)	266.2 (33.4)	-114.6 (32.4)	-30.1%	0.3%
Agriculture Ponds	2,828.5 (4.1)	2,980.8 (3.9)	152.4 (25.3)	5.4%	2.9%
Industrial Ponds	373.4 (17.5)	410.5 (16.4)	37.1 (29.7)	9.9%	0.4%
Natural Ponds	2,103.5 (11.3)	2,088.8 (11.4)	-14.7 (*)	-0.7%	2.0%
Urban Ponds	816.1 (6.3)	963.0 (6.2)	147.0 (12.9)	18.0%	0.9%
Freshwater Ponds	6,502.1 (4.6)	6,709.3 (4.5)	207.2 (29.6)	3.2%	6.4%
All Freshwater Wetlands	104,252.7 (2.8)	104,274.6 (2.8)	21.9 (*)	0.0%	–

* Statistically unreliable.

Percent coefficient of variation was expressed as (standard deviation/mean) × 100.

Freshwater Emergent Marshes

The acreage of freshwater emergent marsh increased by an estimated 1.0 percent between 2004 and 2009. There was a net gain of an estimated 267,800 acres (108,400 ha). These gains resulted principally from wetland reestablishment or creation on upland agricultural lands and lands of other unspecified land use (primarily idle or set-aside lands with no discernible land use type). There were an estimated 367,000 acres (148,600 ha) of freshwater marsh gain from these two upland land use categories and these findings coincided with estimates that more than 59 percent of wetland gains occurred on agricultural lands between 1997 and 2007 (USDA 2010). Although freshwater marshes sustained some losses to urban and rural development (collectively 17,200 acres or 7,000 ha) and silviculture operations (28,500 acres or 11,500 ha), the increases noted above resulted in a net gain in acreage. Some of the gains in wetland emergents also came from areas previously classified as forested wetlands. If forested wetlands were clear cut but the hydrology remained, they were reclassified as emergent wetland. An estimated 421,000 acres of forested wetland were changed to emergent wetlands between 2004 and 2009.

The opposite was true for shrub wetlands as an estimated 570,600 acres of emergent marsh became shrub wetland. Natural succession may account for some of this change, however, drier conditions particularly in the southeastern United States likely promoted shrub growth. Some shrub growth in emergent wetlands also was the result of re-planting pine saplings following clear-cuts for silviculture. The interchange between freshwater emergent marsh wetland and other wetland and upland types is shown in Figure 41.

Losses of freshwater marsh also outdistanced gains in certain portions of the country including the prairie pothole region States of North Dakota, South Dakota, Minnesota, and Iowa. Emergent wetland area also declined in other Midwestern States including Nebraska, Kansas, Missouri, Indiana, Wisconsin, and Michigan. Losses were observed in the Lower Mississippi Alluvial Plain States of Arkansas, Mississippi, and Louisiana and the southeastern States of North Carolina, South Carolina, Georgia, Florida, and Alabama.

Efforts to improve drainage of farm fields as a result of economic and climatic conditions were factors that influenced the loss of freshwater marshes in agricultural areas. Increased drainage in portions of the upper Midwest attempted to eliminate excess water from cropped areas and renewed interest and installation of subsurface drain tile as replacement of aging subsurface drainage systems effectively drained some wetlands (Blann *et al.* 2009). Additionally, acres enrolled in agriculture conservation programs were reduced. Land area in the Conservation Reserve Program (CRP) shrunk in 2007 and 2008 as farmers opted in favor of planting crops to take advantage of high prices for corn and soybeans (Miller 2008). In 2007, CRP acreage in North Dakota declined by 12.4 percent (North Dakota Game and Fish Dept. 2008). Incentives for corn production as part of biofuel programs (the vast majority of United States based ethanol is produced from corn) also encouraged agricultural producers to put additional acreage into row crop production.

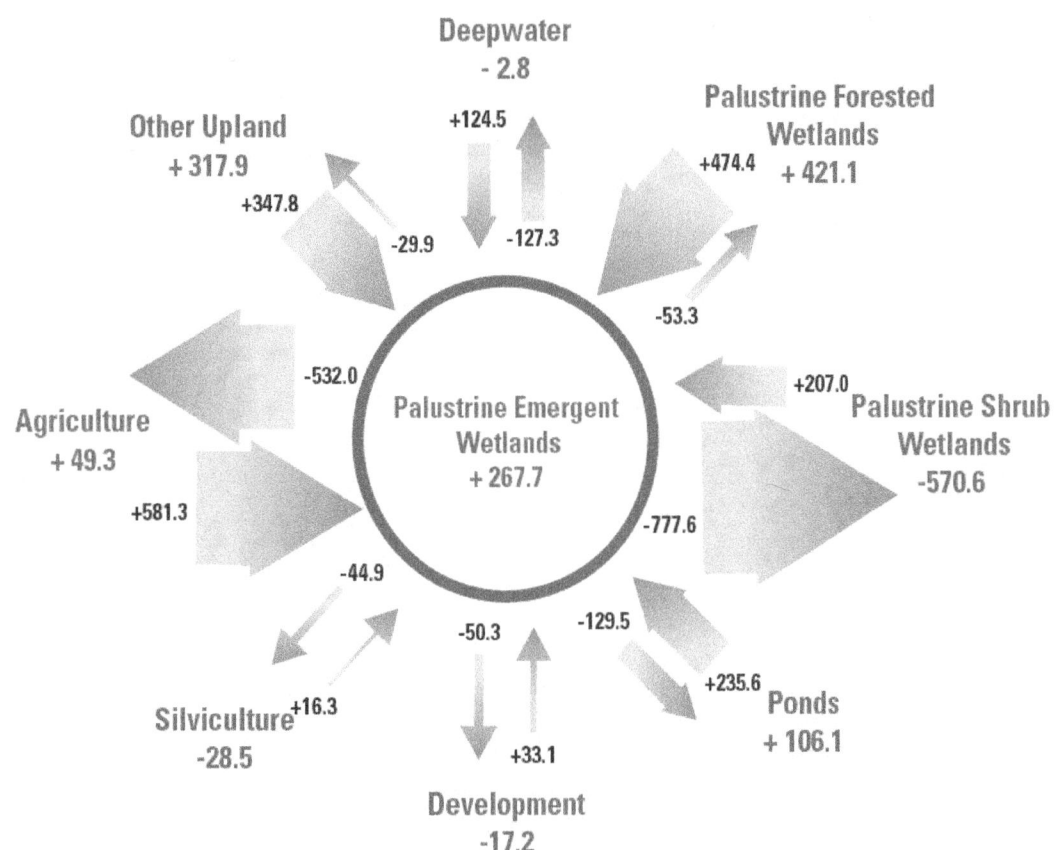

Deepwater
- 2.8

+124.5

-29.9 -127.3

Other Upland
+ 317.9

+347.8

Palustrine Forested
Wetlands
+474.4 + 421.1

-53.3

-532.0

Palustrine Emergent
Wetlands
+ 267.7

+207.0 Palustrine Shrub
Wetlands
-570.6

Agriculture
+ 49.3

+581.3

-777.6

-44.9

-50.3 -129.5

Silviculture +16.3

-28.5

+33.1

+235.6 Ponds
+ 106.1

Development
-17.2

Figure 41. Acreage immigration and emigration of freshwater emergent wetland, 2004 to 2009 (all numbers are in thousands of acres). Arrows indicate the estimated acreage lost and gained between upland, deepwater, and other wetland categories. The interchanges shown in this graphic have resulted primarily from human actions over the 4.5 years covered by this study.

Freshwater emergent wetland, Indiana, 2009.

Freshwater Shrub Wetlands

Freshwater shrubs increased in area by an estimated 180,100 acres (72,900 ha). This net gain came primarily from freshwater emergent wetlands as shown in Figure 42. Shrub wetlands were composed of true shrub species as well as tree saplings less than 20 ft tall (6 m). Representative wetland communities composed of true shrub species included Carolina Bays, pocosins, true shrub swamps, ericaceous shrub bogs, and others (Figure 43). Many wetlands classified as shrub were representatives of

this latter category and in areas of active silviculture management. Consequently, wetland shrub areas that contained tree species have been subject to substantial change corresponding to managed forest harvest rotations as seen in longer term trend information shown in Figure 44.

There was relatively little natural succession of shrub wetlands leading to mature forested wetland as originally envisioned by Cowardin *et al.* (1979). Small pine trees as part of managed pine plantations

matured to become larger pine trees in areas that retained wetland hydrological characteristics. These areas become economically mature and are used for their wood products before they become ecologically mature (deMaynadier and Hunter 1995). An estimated 142,600 acres (57,730 ha) of freshwater shrub wetland were lost (drained or filled) to become upland silviculture between 2004 and 2009.

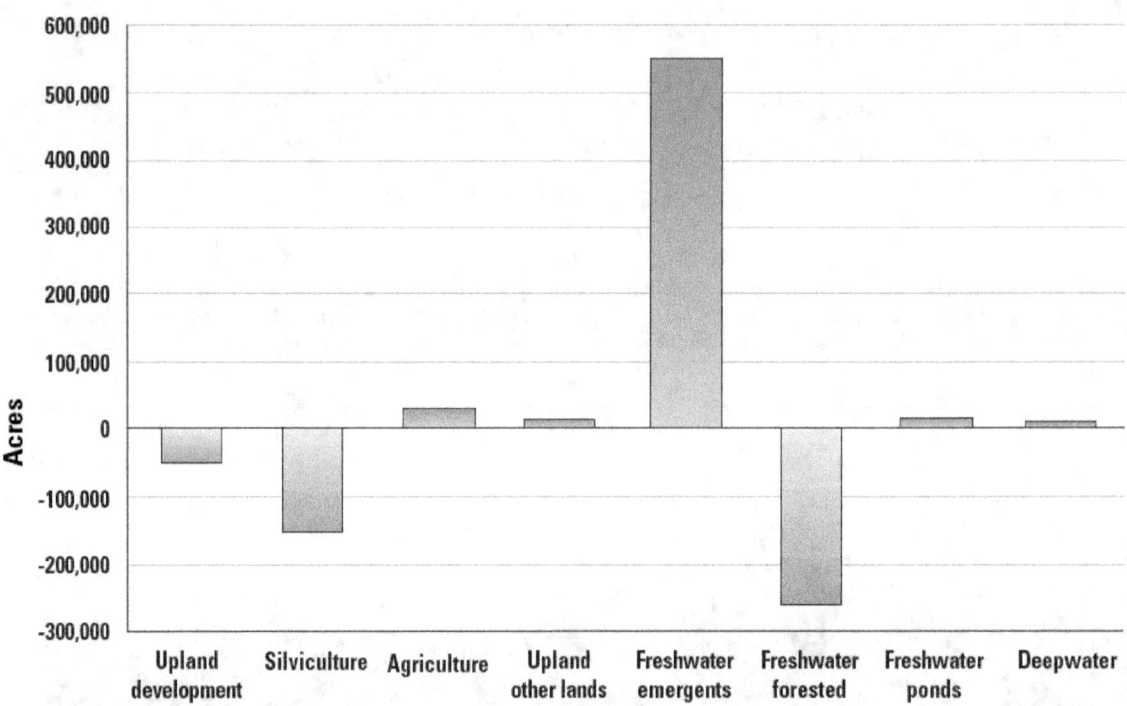

Figure 42. Gains and losses of selected wetland, upland, and deepwater categories that influenced a net gain of freshwater shrub wetland 2004 to 2009.

Figure 43. A freshwater shrub wetland composed of true shrub species, Tennessee (Photograph by St. Mary's University of Minnesota).

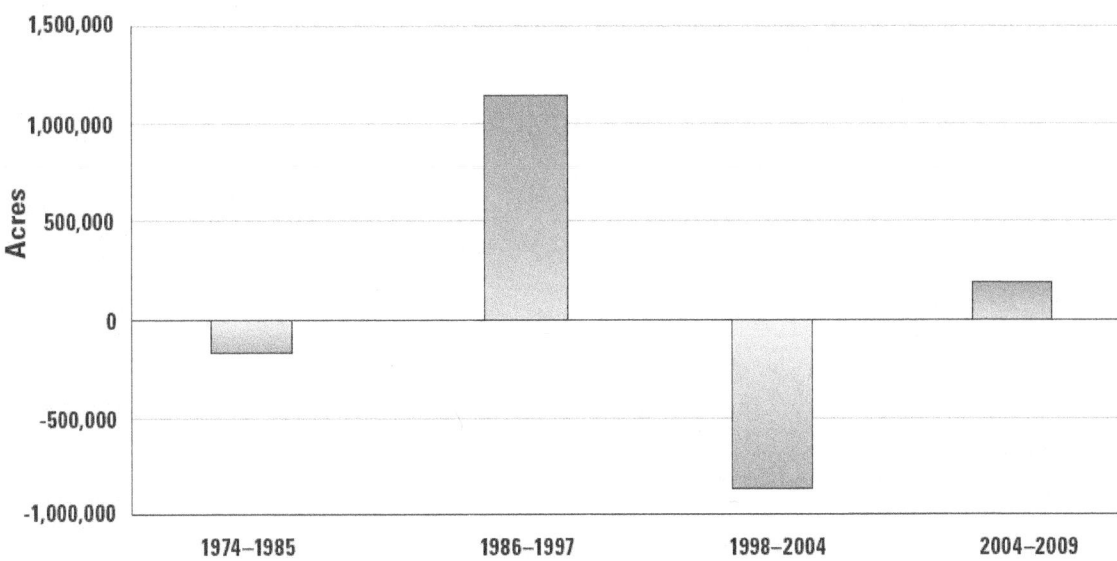

Figure 44. Long-term trends in freshwater shrub net changes, 1974 to 2009. Fluctuation in the rate of change over time was related to silviculture cut and replant cycles in wetland areas. Sources: Dahl and Johnson 1991; Dahl 2000; 2006; and this study.

Freshwater Forested Wetlands

Forested wetlands are ecologically important systems and represent some of the most diverse, complex, and productive freshwater wetlands in the Nation. They also are dynamic, experiencing changes in area, ecological condition, and successional stage over time.

Between 2004 and 2009, forested wetlands declined by an estimated 633,100 acres (256,320 ha). Forested wetlands experienced the largest change in area of any wetland type and reversed a trend where area had increased in the previous two eras of monitoring (Figure 45). Forty-one percent of all freshwater vegetated wetland losses were forested wetlands in the southeastern States of North Carolina, South Carolina, Georgia, Florida, Alabama, Mississippi, Louisiana, and Arkansas. Much of this was the result of change to other wetland types such as freshwater shrubs or emergent wetland resulting from clear-cuts associated with silviculture.

Urban and rural development accounted for 26 percent or an estimated 102,400 acres (41,460 ha) of the forested wetlands losses to uplands. This area represented irreversible losses as wetlands have been filled, drained or otherwise developed for buildings or other support infrastructure. Historically, once these areas have been developed there is very little opportunity for wetland reestablishment and even less chance of successfully restoring mature forested wetlands.

Silviculture accounted for the greatest percentage of the losses to upland between 2004 and 2009. An estimated 149,500 acres (60,500 ha) of forested wetland were lost to silviculture primarily in the Southeastern United States. The pulse in silviculture activity corresponds to a cycle of 20 to 25 year rotation cuts (Jackson 2006; North Carolina State University [NCSU] 2008) common in the Southeastern United States. Timber products from southeastern wetlands include Pond Cypress (*Taxodium ascendens*) used for

sawtimber and landscape mulch (Wear and Greis 2002); bald cypress (*Taxodium distichum*) widely used as mulch in professional landscaping and yards (Beauchamp 1996) but also used for exterior siding, boat docks, outdoor decks and fences; black gum or black tupelo (*Nyssa sylvatica*) used for pallets, rough floors, and pulpwood; and various wetland hardwood species used for furniture-grade wood and veneer.

Although the tree removal process itself did not constitute wetland loss[22], a number of activities related to the timber removal resulted in more permanent changes. Some activities associated with forest plantations involved intensive site preparations and timber stand management practices that altered or eliminated site hydrology (Figure 46). Many of the forested plantations in the southeastern

---

[22] A wetland was not considered lost unless there was sufficient artificial drainage, ditching or filling to effectively remove hydrology. Removal of tree canopy without hydrologic alteration resulted in change in wetland classification (i.e. forest to shrub or emergent wetland).

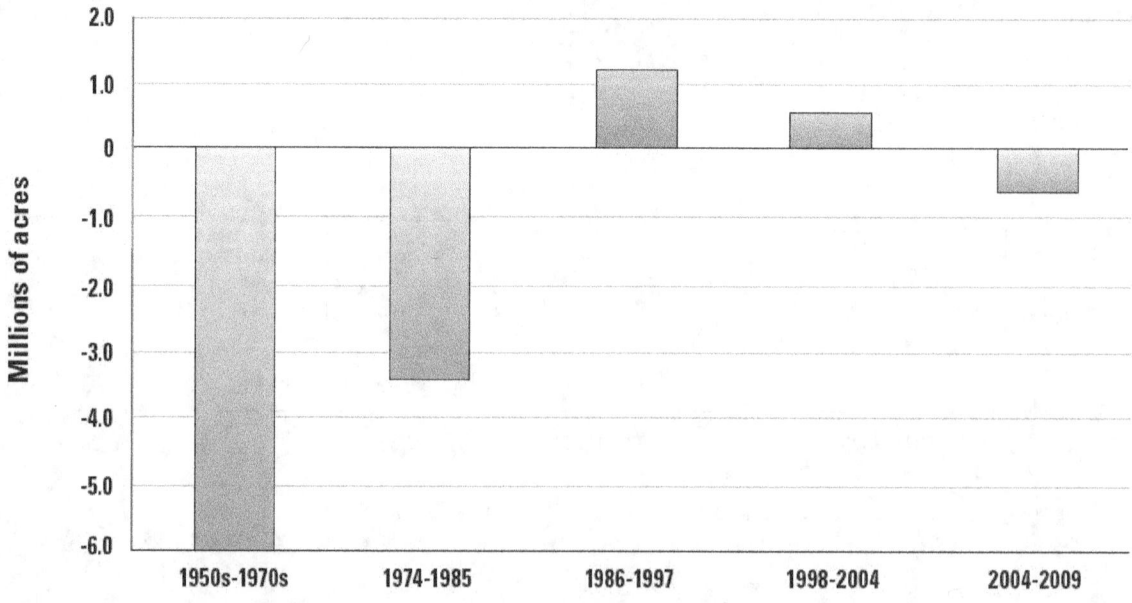

Figure 45. Long-term trends in forested wetland area as measured since the 1950s. Sources: Frayer et al. 1983; Dahl and Johnson 1991; Dahl 2000; 2006; and this study.

United States are even-aged stands dominated by a single species of conifer, typically loblolly pine (*Pinus taeda*), (Miller *et al.* 2003). It has been estimated that loblolly-shortleaf pine forests cover 55 million acres in the Southern States (Smith *et al.* 2009). By design, these plantations had relatively low diversity (deMaynadier and Hunter 1995) and specific management practices included clear cutting, stump and woody debris removal, ditching, drainage and bedding. Specific actions that were deleterious to wetlands included construction of forest roads required to access cut timber sites (deMaynadier and Hunter 1995; Harms *et al.* 1998); installation of drainage ditches through a wetland (Sharitz and Greshan 1998; Wear and Greis 2002); bedding of sites; subsurface drainage; and levee construction, filling, and channelization.

Under Section 404 of the Clean Water Act (CWA), a permit is not required for the discharge of dredged or fill material associated with normal silviculture activities or the construction of and maintenance of forest roads. However, the CWA and implementing regulations indicate that activities in wetlands that convert "waters of the United States" to upland always require authorization under Section 404. The implementing regulations provided "Best Management Practices" (BMPs) for the construction or maintenance of forest roads that must be adhered to in ensuring adverse effects on the aquatic environment are minimized. In the 1990s, Federal and State regulatory agencies, the forestry community and the public began to recognize that mechanical silvicultural operations were having measurable and "significant" impacts on aquatic ecosystems. Federal guidance was developed to clarify circumstances where mechanical silvicultural site preparation activities would and would not require a permit under Section 404 of the CWA (USEPA 2010b). As a result, mechanical silvicultural site preparation activities for the establishment of pine plantations in the Southeast should require a permit for activities in certain forested wetland types including cypress-gum swamps, muck and peat swamps, cypress strands and domes, seasonally flooded (or wetter) bottomland hardwood wetlands, Carolina Bays, white cedar swamps, seasonally flooded (or wetter) forested wetlands on riverine floodplains and some very poorly drained non-riverine forested wetlands (USEPA 2010b). However, other areas including seasonally, intermittently or temporarily flooded or saturated forested wetlands do not require a permit for mechanical silvicultural site preparation activities.

Also excluded from permit requirements were forested wetlands that support 25 percent or greater canopy of pine including pine/hardwood forests and pine/

Figure 46. This drainage ditch (foreground) effectively altered wetland hydrology and was still functional several years following development of this pine plantation.

Figure 47. Both long-leaf (Pinus palustris) and slash pine (Pinus elliottii) occur naturally in southeastern wetlands. The forested wetland pictured here has greater than 25 percent canopy of long-leaf and slash pine. Under existing Federal guidance, these wetland types have been exempted from requirements for a regulatory permit for mechanical silviculture site preparation activities.

cypress wetlands. These exclusions apply to pine flatwood wetlands, seepage forests, saturated hammocks, pond pine woodland, and forested wet flats (Figure 47).

To better assess the cumulative effects of intensive silviculture operations requires consideration of past regional hydrologic modifications (including regional development patterns) and how that may be interacting with climatic changes to accentuate wetland loss resulting from actions such as "minor drainage" or other "normal silviculture operations." For example, recent research has suggested that forest removal and climate change (i.e., warming and drying) would have pronounced impacts on the groundwater table during the dry periods in cypress wetland managed upland pine stands (Lu *et al.* 2009).

A number of authors (Capel *et al.* 1995; Allen *et al.* 1996; Bliss and Comerford 2002; Jackson 2006;

and others) have identified issues related to the impacts of extensive pine plantations on important ecological functions. Some of the issues recognized include: lack of diversity in tree species planted and conversion from hardwood and mixed stand types to mono-specific stands of pine; extensive alteration of habitat by timber removal (clear cuts); extensive acreage in single or similar age-class plantations; and wetland drainage or hydrologic modifications such as skidder created ditches that can widen over time and drain wetlands.

A recent EPA review of south Atlantic coastal wetlands also highlighted the uncertainties surrounding the potential impacts of forestry practices on wetlands (USEPA unpublished). Even when BMPs for silviculture operations are followed, wetland habitats and community structure may still be seriously degraded (NCSU 2008) and forested wetland functions adversely affected (Wear and Greis 2002). Wetland substrates

are often not suited to support heavy equipment used for forestry operations. This disruption in combination with canopy removal from timber harvest has had a substantial impact on wetland functions and physical habitat structure (Figure 48). Forestry activity such as clear cuts adjacent to wetlands also can affect wetland habitat by altering input of sunlight, nutrients and sediment (Jackson 2006), an important concept since approximately 45 percent of all forested wetlands sampled in this study were within or adjacent to areas classified as forested plantations (silviculture).

Wetland areas that were re-planted as part of a managed silviculture operation could not be distinguished from those that had been re-planted as part of a wetland restoration effectively masking estimates of reestablishment of forested wetlands. However, there have been increased attempts to reestablish some wetland hardwood areas in the Southeastern United States

Figure 48. A former forested wetland in South Carolina one year following clear-cut. (Photograph by M. Bergeson, USFWS.)

mostly on former agricultural lands (De Steven 2009; Gardiner and Oliver 2005). The "Bottomland Timber Establishment on Wetlands" initiative of the U.S. Department of Agriculture's (USDA) Farm Service Agency (FSA) through the Conservation Reserve Program may increase those restoration efforts (USDA 2007).

Additional Analysis of Recent Changes

Over the intervals of time covered by this series of wetlands status and trends reports, policy and resource management decisions have had various effects on the legal, financial, and regulatory tools designed to influence conservation and land use policy in the United States. Most notable examples include the Coastal Zone Management Act of 1972 (P.L. 92-583, 16 U.S.C. 1451-1456); the Clean Water Act of 1977 and amendments (P.L. 95-217); the conservation provisions of the Food Security Act (Farm Bill) of 1985 and subsequent versions; the Tax Reform Act of 1986 (P.L. 99-514, 100 Stat. 2085); the Emergency Wetlands Resources Act of 1986 (P.L. 99-645, 100 Stat. 3582); the North American Wetlands Conservation Act of 1989 (P.L. 101-233); the Partners for Fish and Wildlife Act of 2006 (P.L. 109–294, 120 Stat. 1351); and others.

Decisions by the Supreme Court in 2001 (Solid Waste Management Agencies of Northern Cook County v. United States Army Corps of Engineers [531 U.S. 159 - SWANCC], and again in 2006 (Rapanos *et ux., et al.* v. United States, 126 S. Ct. 2208) narrowed the prior interpretation of the scope of waters protected by the Clean Water Act and Federal agencies (Zinn and Copeland 2007). The effects of those decisions are most applicable to some freshwater wetland types and although the impacts of those rulings may not be fully recognized for some time, there has been considerable debate about the consequences they may have to wetland resources (Chertok and Sinding 2005; Copeland 2010). At a minimum, there has been a perception that the Federal role in wetland regulation has been diminished and some types of freshwater wetlands are no longer included under Federal regulatory mechanisms (Ruffolo 2002: Downing *et al.* 2003; Williams and Connolly 2005; Cain 2008).

Tying wetland losses to any particular policy, action or governmental decision does not always have a clear linkage as there have been contributing considerations such as economic conditions (i.e., crop prices or property values), land use trends and climatic changes that have the potential to influence changes in wetland area.

Past studies have demonstrated that some regional trends in wetland change can be contrary to national trends. Stedman and Dahl (2008) found that even though the Nation experienced a net gain in wetland area, losses of freshwater wetlands in the coastal watersheds along the Atlantic and Gulf of Mexico contributed to net losses on a regional basis between 1998 and 2004. Regions of more extensive wetland losses or gains have existed based on many factors and while this study showed wetland changes were widely distributed (all 48 States), certain regions of the country have experienced higher wetland loss rates. Geospatial analyses of the data from 2004 to 2009 provided further insights to regional wetland loss patterns and these are depicted in Figure 49.

Bedford (1999) recognized that irreversible loss of wetland resulted from some types of extensive development such as urbanization, the construction of airports, harbors and other infrastructure. In localized areas, wetland losses due to human alteration have become so pervasive that changes to regional hydrology threaten the sustainability of the remaining wetland area and constrain possible opportunities for future reestablishment.

Figure 49. This study found particular regions of the conterminous United States experienced different rates of wetland loss depending on many factors. The regions illustrated on the map experienced the highest rate of freshwater wetland loss to upland between 2004 and 2009. (This examination was based on geospatial analysis of data from this study. There may be no statistical relevance attached to any region(s) depicted.) NOTE: This information was intended to illustrate the observed incidence of higher wetland loss rates by generalized region. It should not minimize the importance of other wetland loss or gain actions that occurred elsewhere.

Figure 50 illustrates the extent of cumulative wetland losses in a rapidly developing area from 1998 to 2009. Hydrologic fragmentation (Figure 51) influences how wetlands function as landscape components and may require re-evaluation of wetland protection, conservation, mitigation, and reestablishment programs in specific watersheds or physiographic settings. In these instances, previously employed wetland management techniques are no longer appropriate because they do not account for collective influences on the ecosystem (Euliss *et al.* 2008). Evaluating the consequences of multiple disturbances or cumulative impacts on wetlands in watersheds or broader landscape level systems is something that has required additional consideration for some time (Bedford and Preston 1988).

Figures 50 A. Originally, approximately 93 percent of the land area pictured was vegetated wetland with level, poorly drained or very poorly drained hydric soils[23] (NRCS 2010) typical of the sloughs and wet flatwoods of south Florida (Liudahl et al. 1989). Areas shaded in orange illustrate the extent of wetland loss between 1998 and 2004. There were 668 acres (270 ha) of observed wetland losses all attributed to development over that 6 year period. All wetlands lost in this example were freshwater wetland types. (Total land area pictured was approximately 4.0 mi² [10.4 km²] and is displayed on 2007 aerial imagery.

[23] Hydric soils are those soils that are saturated, flooded or ponded long enough during the growing season for the development of anaerobic conditions in the topsoil. The anaerobic conditions in a hydric soil favor the growth and regeneration of hydrophytic vegetation.

Figure 50 B. Updated loss information showing cumulative wetland losses 1998 to 2004 (displayed in orange) and 2004 to 2009 (displayed in light green). An additional 290 acres (117 ha) of wetland area was lost over a 4.5 year period as documented by this study. The impacts of wetland losses have resulted in further fragmentation of the original hydrologic system and the remaining wetland area in this vicinity must be considered imminently threatened by future development.

Figure 51. Remnant cypress (Taxodium sp.) remain as part of a former forested wetland complex in south Florida. Extensive urban development (fill for housing) has resulted in hydrologic fragmentation of a broader wetland complex and has imposed constraints on any reestablishment efforts (also see Figures 50 A and 50 B).

Wetland Restoration, Reestablishment,[24] and Creation

Between 2004 and 2009, reestablishment of wetland area was attributed to actions on agriculture lands and "other" lands with undetermined land use (refer to Figure 22 in the Results section). An estimated 489,600 acres (198,230 ha) of former upland were re-classified as wetland. There also should be acknowledgment of other wetland enhancement projects that did not increase acreage but sought to improve wetland quality and were not assessed as part of this study.

The primary motivation for many wetland reestablishment efforts has been the substantial losses of wetland area that has occurred through the cumulative actions of numerous individual decisions that altered or destroyed wetlands (Bedford 1999). Reestablishment and enhancement programs have been bolstered by shifts during the late 1980s and into the 1990s to redirect Federal policy away from regulation to an incentive-based approach to reduce losses and encourage conservation or reestablishment of wetland areas. In recent years, programs such as USDA's Wetlands and Conservation Reserve Programs; the Fish and Wildlife Service's North American Waterfowl and Wetlands Management Plan, the Partners for Fish and Wildlife Program, Coastal Program and the National Wildlife Refuge System; the U.S. Army Corps of Engineer's Aquatic Ecosystem Restoration Program; EPA's National Estuary Program; and others worked in tandem with landowners and other management programs to conserve, protect, enhance or reestablish wetland resources (Council on Environmental Quality 2008).

---

[24] This report defined wetland reestablishment as the restoration of wetland characteristics on a former wetland site.

An example of a successful collaborative effort to reestablish wetland acreage has been provided by Ducks Unlimited and is presented as a Case Study (see inset). This and other wetland reestablishment efforts have been reflected in an overall decline in the net rate of wetland loss, particularly on agricultural lands. Estuarine wetlands that were outside the scope of many agricultural conservation measures have not benefited from the broad scale reestablishment programs that have been successful in increasing inland wetland extent on a national level.[25]

Over time, wetland losses have occurred where land use changes converted wetlands for other purposes, most notably some form of human use (Dahl and Johnson 1991; Dahl 2005). Since the 1950s, there has been an estimated 700,000 acres (283,400 ha) of intertidal wetland; 19 million acres (7.7 million ha) of forested wetland; and 7.0 million acres (2.8 million ha) of emergent wetlands drained or otherwise lost. These patterns of wetland loss have not occurred randomly on the landscape (Dahl and Allord 1996; Bedford 1999) and it follows that wetland restoration (the process of reestablishment of an area that was once wetland) also does not occur at random. Federal resource agencies sponsoring wetland reestablishment projects have to consider programmatic priorities, willing landowner participation, available funding and technological

challenges presented by restoration science. As a consequence, the pragmatic approach has been to focus efforts on less intensively developed lands (i.e., agricultural lands) as opportunities have arisen to restore or enhance drained or degraded wetlands. Rarely have wetlands been reestablished in intensively developed areas (i.e., near shopping malls, urbanized developments, coastal developments, or similar areas). Reestablishment also has been less common in tidal wetlands or in areas where land values or engineering constraints have made these projects more costly (Stedman and Dahl 2008). The concept that some existing degraded wetland(s) may not be restorable because of landscape-level changes to hydrology is further complicated by potential changes in climate and how those changes may affect precipitation, temperature, and evaporation. The trends in where and what types of wetlands have been reestablished have implications for national policy goals, wetland biodiversity and, to some extent, geospatial distribution.

Mitigation for wetland losses, wetland reestablishment, and creation are forms of resource management aimed at curtailing acreage losses and hopefully improving wetland condition. These programs have been successful at increasing the area of wetland reestablished on a national level (Dahl 2006); however, these same

programs have affected the diversity of wetland type(s) and spatial distribution locally and regionally. Some types of wetlands, such as freshwater emergent marshes and open water ponds, have been preferentially reestablished or created, whereas replacement of forested wetlands (a type that has experienced some of the greatest losses), has lagged behind and other types of wetlands including bogs and fens are seldom, if ever successfully replaced (Kentula 1996; Gorham and Rochefort 2003). Other studies have demonstrated that there continues to be non-parity between wetland types that have been lost and subsequent wetland mitigation, reestablishment or creation actions (Kentula et al. 1992; Mitsch and Wilson 1996; Brooks et al. 2005; Biebighauser 2007; Kudray and Schemm 2008). The net effect has been the loss of wetland diversity, hydrologic function, biological communities, and a "homogenization of wetland landscapes" (Bedford 1996, 1999). Wetlands as important hydrologic components on the landscape should be viewed in context with large-scale hydrologic systems. Changes in precipitation, surface water inputs and outflows, drainage patterns, and flow all influence the biophysical processes. Cogent to this discussion has been the issue of freshwater pond construction as replacement for lost wetlands.

[25] Discrete projects have realized tidal wetland reestablishment but have been limited in scope. Currently, the Coastal Wetlands Planning, Protection, and Restoration Act is attempting some larger scale reestablishment of tidal wetlands in Louisiana.

Case Study

Ducks Unlimited (DU) delivers conservation throughout North America. DU's habitat protection and restoration efforts focus on retaining and reestablishing wetland habitat and wetland functions. One such wetland reestablishment project in west-central Mississippi was completed in 2006 by DU for the Natural Resource Conservation Service (NRCS) Wetland Reserve Program (WRP) and has been chronicled by the series of photographs below.

This area of the Lower Mississippi River Alluvial Plain provides essential winter habitat for waterfowl and is the most important area for wintering mallards (Anas platyrhynchos) in North America (Davis and Afton 2010). Historically, this area was subject to flooding events on rivers and tributaries that greatly influenced the landscape, producing a surface geomorphology comprised of natural depressions, meander scar (oxbow) lakes, and relatively flat topography (Dahl et al. 2009). Seasonal flooding and localized ponding on poorly drained soils maintained the wetlands (Showalter and Spigener 2008), however, a number of studies have documented the precipitous decline of wetlands over time in this region of Mississippi (Turner et al. 1981; Heitmeyer et al. 1989; Harris and Gosselink 1990).

Approximately 543 acres (220 ha) that had been in agricultural production were restored to wetland as part of this project (see sequential reestablishment figures). Nearly 120 acres (48 ha) of emergent wetland habitat were created in five impounded areas. To augment this marsh reestablishment, surrounding areas were planted with bottomland hardwood tree species in the spring of 2006. The afforestation of bottomland hardwood sites in the Lower Mississippi Alluvial Valley is vital as less than one percent of the original forested area has been restored (Schoenholtz et al. 2001).

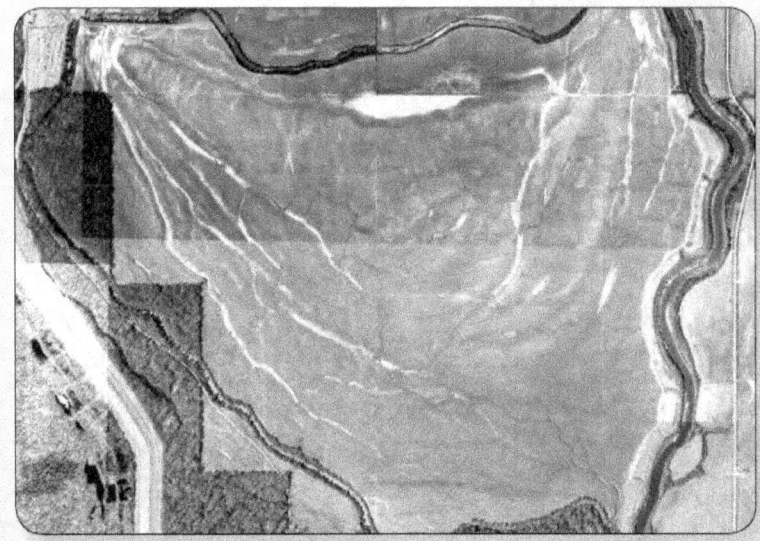

A 1996 black and white image of the Ducks Unlimited project area prior to reestablishment. At the time this image was captured, the area was in agricultural production.

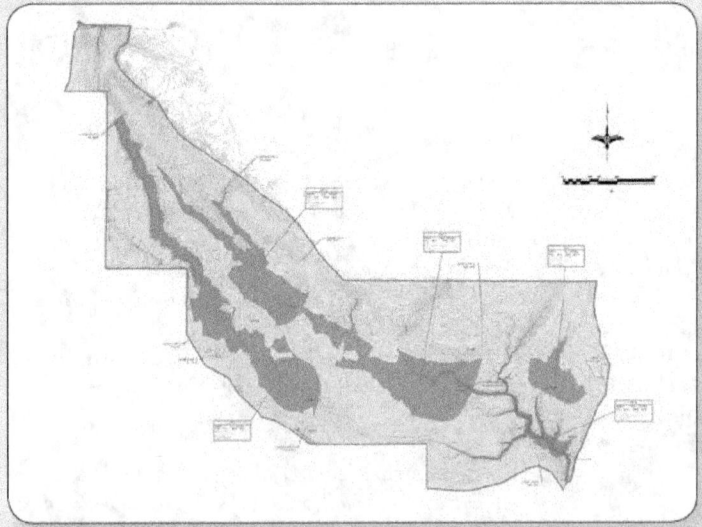

A topographic survey map aids with details of the project area and engineering (courtesy of Ducks Unlimited, Inc.)

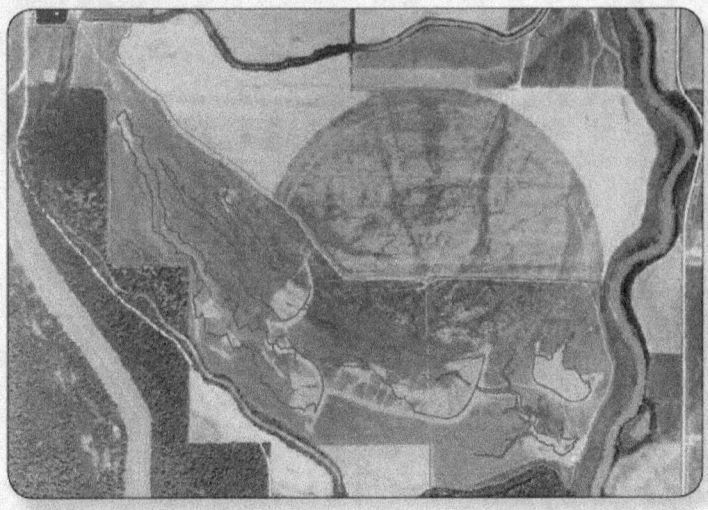

September, 2006. This true color image shows the progress of converting agricultural lands to emergent wetlands. Blue lines outline the five impoundments corresponding to the engineering plans for this reestablishment.

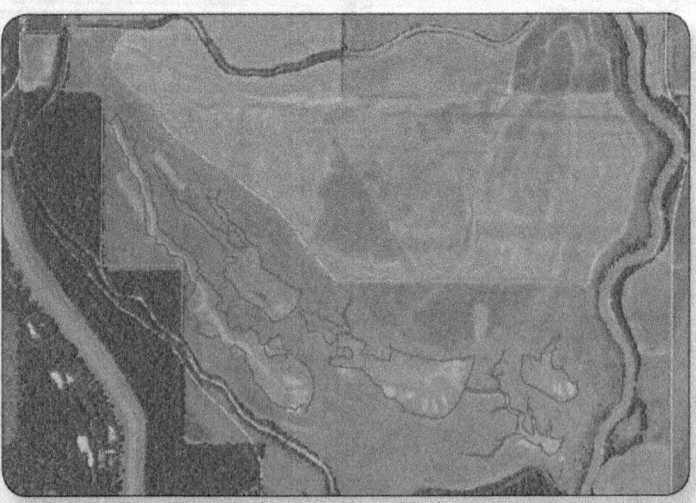

2009 imagery showing the completed reestablishment project (outlined in red). This resulted in a gain of 574.8 acres (233 ha) of emergent wetland.

Information provided courtesy of Ducks Unlimited Inc.

Tracking Wetland Reestablishment

Tracking wetland reestablishment accomplishments by acreage is important to accurately determine wetland extent and location, however, challenges remain due to lack of coordination between tracking and reporting systems, overlapping partnerships and over-reporting acreages associated with wetland reestablishment projects (CEQ 2008). As an example of acreage tracking issues, analysis of wetland reestablishment projects in Wisconsin was conducted in conjunction with USFWS, EPA, the Center for Urban Watershed Renewal and Virginia Polytechnic Institute and State University (Roghair 2009). Initial geospatial data from that study was used to further examine wetland reestablishment project areas in detail. As shown in Figure 52,

using the total project area resulted in over-reporting acreage accomplishments. This was attributed to a lack of geospatial wetland boundary information within the project area that would have properly identified pre-existing wetland area (not attributable as wetland acreage gains), reestablished wetland area and type(s) and any upland included within the project. Tabular or narrative reporting of wetland reestablishment acreage has led to confusion over the actual number of wetland acres gained versus reporting of total project area. Geospatial information on the extent and type of wetland reestablished is needed if future reestablishment information is intended to contribute to monitoring wetland acreage gains.

 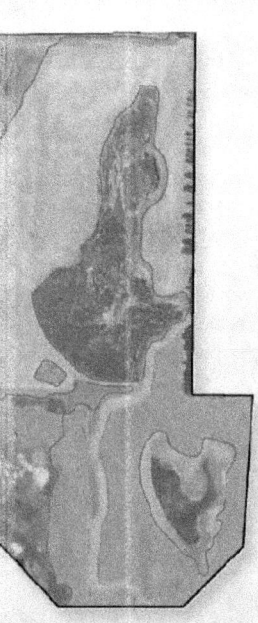 

1996   **2008**

☐ Existing Wetlands – 11 acres*
☐ Reestablished Wetlands – 35 acres
☐ Uplands – 75 acres*

Figure 52. This series of image maps illustrate the end result of a 121 acre (49.0 ha) wetland reestablishment project in southern Wisconsin. Although reported as a 121 acre restoration, the project area was composed of pre-existing wetland (11 acres as outlined in blue on the 1996 image), 35 acres (14.2 ha) of reestablished wetland and 75 acres (30.4 ha) of upland. All wetland areas (pre-existing and reestablished wetland) have been outlined in blue on the 2008 image. Some wetland reestablishment projects fail to identify and record geospatial information on wetland extent and consequently over-report project accomplishments.

Freshwater Ponds

The status and changes between 2004 and 2009 for all freshwater pond types are shown in Table 4. There was a net increase of 207,200 acres (83,890 ha) of freshwater ponds between 2004 and 2009 and this contributed to the 3.2 percent increase in the extent of freshwater wetland ponds nationally. Past practices of replacing lost wetlands (of any type) with small permanent ponds has been discouraged and supposedly replaced with required mitigation plans that replace functions (Batzer and Sharitz 2006). Many storm water ponds, for example, are considered by planners as a valid solution to the problem of wetland habitat loss (Woodcock *et al.* 2010). Data from this study indicated that freshwater pond creation outdistanced increases of most other wetland types (except freshwater emergent) and continued to be a component of wetland restoration and creation strategies.

Certain subcategories of ponds exhibited area losses. Aquaculture ponds declined in area by an estimated 114,560 acres (46,380 ha). This occurred primarily in the Lower Mississippi Valley where catfish farm pond numbers were affected by dynamics in the domestic catfish market. Grain prices for feed, energy costs and lending

institutions unable to provide capital to growers based on depressed prices for catfish contributed to this change in the extent of aquaculture ponds. Production of catfish had dropped from 660 million pounds to a projected 380 million pounds over the course of several years and the number of catfish (aquaculture) ponds declined in response as some were abandoned or converted to row crops (Heartland 2008). However, provisions enacted in the Farm Bill have allowed catfish farmers to enlist ponds into the Conservation Reserve Program (Phillips 2008). As a result, considerable acreage of aquaculture ponds were drained or left idle and there were an estimated 43,750 acres (17,710 ha) of aquaculture ponds that were re-classified as emergent wetland between 2004 and 2009 (Figure 53). It was not possible to distinguish between ponds that were part of the Conservation Reserve Program and ponds that had been otherwise idled.

There was a decline of 14,700 acres (5,950 ha), or less than 1.0 percent, in ponds exhibiting natural characteristics. Most of these changes resulted from successional changes such as abandonment of beaver impoundments or natural succession to wetland emergents or shrubs.

Open water wetlands classified as urban ponds increased by an estimated 18 percent in area between 2004 and 2009. The continued increase in urban ponds was the result of multiple factors including wetland drainage into centralized water retention basins; new ponds created to comply with water runoff requirements; and ponds constructed for recreational purposes. Building codes and other ordinances often required runoff water retention[26] to compensate for areas of impervious surface construction (Figure 54). Constructed urban runoff wetlands and multiple-pond systems have been used to remove pollutants by detaining flows that lead to sedimentation and have been encouraged as a new development measure to control urban runoff (USEPA 2010e). Ponds and small lakes also tended to increase property values and were preferred by homeowners (Doss and Taff 1996).

Ponds on agricultural lands increased by an estimated 5.4 percent or 152,400 acres (61,700 ha). Some of these were water bodies used for on-farm purposes such as dug-outs for livestock watering. Others were the result of wetland reestablishment or creation efforts stemming from conservation measures.

---

[26] EPA has defined *Constructed urban runoff wetlands*: Those wetlands that are intentionally created on sites that are not wetlands for the primary purpose of wastewater or urban runoff treatment and are managed as such. Constructed wetlands are normally considered as part of the urban runoff collection and treatment system (USEPA 2010d).

Figure 53. Former aquaculture ponds in west-central Mississippi (shown as rectangular shapes) supported wetland emergent plant growth in 2009. Similar catfish ponds were made eligible for the USDA Conservation Reserve Program under the Farm Bill (2009).

Figure 54. A created pond in an urban subdivision has been used to drain an adjacent vegetated wetland and serves as a retention basin to compensate for the increase in impervious surface from the development.

Industrial pond area also increased slightly. Industrial ponds made up only about 6.0 percent of all freshwater pond area in 2009.

Although the assessment of the qualitative aspects of wetlands was beyond the scope of the study, analysis of these data have recognized issues regarding the types of wetlands that have been reestablished or created and the objectives of the policies or programs that potentially influence wetland characteristics and distribution.

There is consensus in the scientific literature that ponds are indeed wetlands (Cowardin et al. 1979; Baldassarre and Bolen 1994; Kentula et al. 2004; Oertli et al. 2005; Batzer and Sharitz 2006; Zedler 2006; Kudray and Schemm 2008) and they support biological diversity (Oertli et al. 2002). As constructed freshwater ponds continue to compensate for area losses in natural wetland acreage, questions regarding these types of wetlands as suitable replacement for lost wetlands continue to be debated.

The widespread geographical nature of where freshwater ponds were created between 2004 and 2009 is shown in Figure 55. The trend of increased pond area has been sustained and has influenced the distribution and types of open water wetlands on the landscape. After examining a large number of wetland "replacement" projects Kentula et al. (1992) concluded that the most common hydrologic pattern adopted for freshwater wetland mitigation was an area of deeper open water surrounded by shallower water with a band of emergent vegetation (Figure 56). This tendency has been commonplace, and in many instances, it was not possible to distinguish ponds constructed as wetland from ponds created for other purposes with similar physical or spatial characteristics. An analysis of constructed ponds over an 11-year period (1998 to 2009) failed to find substantial wetland vegetation had developed to reclassify open-water ponds as another wetland type (e.g., emergent or shrub wetland). This study found that 83 percent of freshwater ponds present in the status and trends survey in 1998 retained open water, pond-like characteristics in 2009.

Whether as mitigation sites, wetland reestablishment, or non-conservation related activities, the construction of open water ponds has continued as evidenced by the findings in this study and others. The Wisconsin Department of Natural Resources found that in Ozaukee County, Wisconsin, the acreage of excavated ponds increased from 96 acres (38.9 ha) in 1979 to 762 acres (308.5 ha) in 2005 (Ozaukee County is the smallest county in Wisconsin [Personal communication, L. Simon,

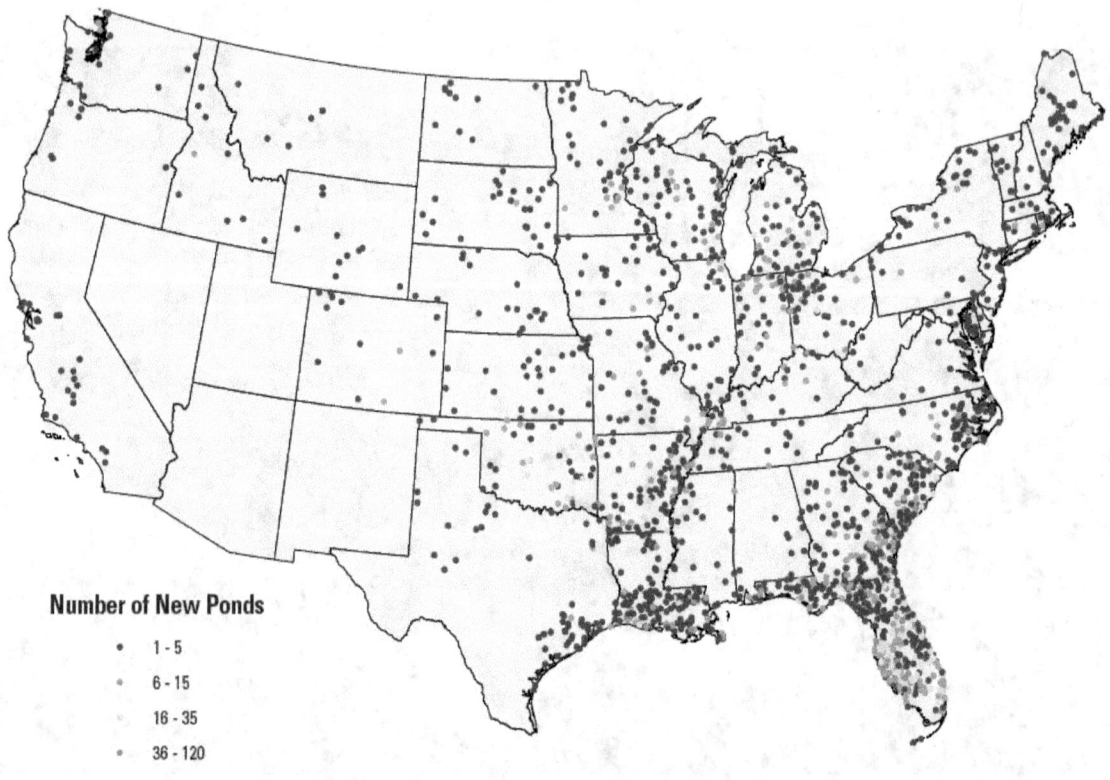

Number of New Ponds

- 1 - 5
- 6 - 15
- 16 - 35
- 36 - 120

Figure 55. Distribution of created ponds in the conterminous United States. Freshwater pond area increased by an estimated 207,000 acres between 2004 and 2009.

Figure 56. Many created wetlands share common characteristics of a deeper open-water basin ringed by a band of emergent vegetation. An estimated 83 percent of these wetlands have remained as open-water basins over time[27].

Wisconsin Dept. Nat. Res. 2010]). In southwestern Montana, 921 created wetlands were almost all small ponds with standing water and had been constructed primarily for recreational use (Kudray and Schemm 2008). In Ohio, updated wetland inventory data show a 44,000 acre (17,800 ha) net increase in open water wetlands that averaged under one acre (2.47 ha) in size (Ducks Unlimited 2009). In some watersheds, open water ponds represent the preponderance of surface water features remaining on the landscape.

Although restored or created wetlands have often been very different than natural wetlands (Whigham 1999), the notion that

open water ponds have been replacement for wetlands has raised questions about resource management programs or policies that have encouraged freshwater pond creation. There are a variety of policies and programs in place at the Federal, State, and local levels that promote (perhaps unknowingly or unintentionally) pond construction. As part of this project, a review of the programs that have provided incentives for the construction of freshwater ponds identified 56 Federal sources for funding and/ or technical assistance. These included such programs as wetland grants, wildlife habitat incentive programs, non-point source implementation grants, watershed rehabilitation programs, flood

prevention programs, and others. Other programs were available to provide public-private partnership arrangements for pond construction (USEPA 2010d). Freshwater ponds have been easy to create (Zedler 2006). Certain types of ponds have been designed to replace wetland functions or habitat, while others have been engineered to provide other physical or societal benefits (e.g., water retention). Freshwater ponds, like many other types of wetlands, have the potential to provide multiple ecological functions as supported by a number of studies (Ruwaldt *et al.* 1979; Lokemoen 1982; Adams *et al.* 1985; White and Martin 2004; Stevens *et al.* 2007; Woodcock *et al.* 2010). However, there also has been ample literature

---

[27] This was determined by a review of created open water ponds identified by this study between 1998 and 2009.

that cited ponds as less desirable. Examples included: Ponds providing lower ecological functions (Kudray and Schemm 2008); accumulation of contaminants in ponds (Barber 2006); heavy metal effects on wildlife (Kennamer et al. 2005); creating environments less favorable for native amphibians or promoting other invasive species (Kentula et al. 2004); and excess nutrient loading (Casey and Klaine 2001).

Bedford (1996) pointed out that replacement wetlands cannot be equivalent to lost wetlands unless their hydrologic features are equivalent. The concept that wetland functions can be replaced by created wetlands has led to targeting a select function as equivalent replacement and constructing a wetland pond specifically to address that targeted function. In this regard, some created wetlands have not been equivalent replacement for natural wetlands that contribute multiple environmental services.

Pond creation and the potential impact on habitat, native species, water quantity, quality and unforeseen physical and ecological processes such as changes in microclimate need additional research to assess positive or negative contributions of these types of wetlands. Currently, there is no clear consensus in scientific literature about constructed ponds providing functional equivalency and there is considerable uncertainty about actual functional contributions due to a lack of research and unpredictable ecological interactions in wetland replacement projects.

"...resource managers may have little understanding of the magnitude of pond creation and the resultant impact on water quantity and quality issues, which are increasingly problematic in Montana and other Western States. The lack of knowledge about the number of ponds being created is amplified by the lack of research quantifying the impact of created ponds on water quantity and quality issues, or other associated positive and negative ecological functions"

Kudray and Schemm 2008

Further examination of the issues regarding continued pond construction and the potential consequences is needed.

Changes in wetland type and extent have provided important information about trends and insights to wetland policy and management applications for the Nation. Assessing the structural properties of wetland landscapes hinges on knowing the extent (number and area), shape and geophysical distribution of wetland types within any particular landscape (Bedford and Preston 1988). However, a more complete assessment of wetlands requires a qualitative aspect to help gage the condition of the remaining wetland resource. The need to address this issue has become more pressing as losses in wetland acreage have largely been compensated by gains in constructed wetland acreage. Data on wetland location, type, surrounding land use and status from this study has provided a baseline for further work to assess wetland condition as conducted by the EPA beginning in 2011 (See special insert: Tracking trends in the quality of the Nation's wetlands).

Tracking Trends in the Quality of the Nation's Wetlands—A Powerful Supplement to Status and Trends

Michael Scozzafava, Mary E. Kentula, Elizabeth Riley, Teresa K. Magee, Lynda Hall, Gregg Serenbetz, Richard Sumner, Chris Faulkner, Myra Price[1]

The U.S. Environmental Protection Agency (EPA), in collaboration with states, tribes, US Fish and Wildlife Service (USFWS), and other federal partners will conduct the first-ever National Wetland Condition Assessment (NWCA) in 2011. This survey is the fifth in a series of National Aquatic Resources Surveys carried out by EPA and state partners to improve understanding of the quality of the Nation's waters. The results of the NWCA will be published in 2013 and repeat surveys will be conducted every five years, resources permitting. The NWCA is designed to build on the success of the USFWS Wetland Status and Trends (S&T) Report. Just as the S&T Report characterizes wetland acreage by category across the conterminous United States, the NWCA will characterize wetland condition nationwide for many of the same wetland classes. When paired together, the two efforts will provide the public and government agencies with comparable, national information on wetland quantity and quality.

Combining wetland quantity and quality data provides a stronger basis for informing effective wetland protection strategies. The wetland quantity information produced by USFWS addresses wetland acreage gained or lost annually, where the greatest gains and losses are occurring, and what wetland types are most vulnerable to loss. The NWCA will provide detailed information on wetland quality by wetland type and area of the country, providing additional clarity into the implications of the acreage gains and losses. Wetland quality or condition speaks to how wetlands differ from the "natural" state, providing an assessment of the overall ecological integrity of the resource and the relative status of wetland processes such as the ability of a wetland to absorb nutrients (Fennessy et al. 2004). In addition, the

stressors most associated with degraded wetland condition will be identified because they provide insights into the causes of declining wetland quality. For example, ditching substantially impacts wetland hydrology, altering plant community composition and the habitat for many wetland-dependent organisms. At the same time, ditches decrease the capacity of wetlands to store storm water because they rapidly move water off site. If ditching is a common practice in a region, the overall ability of the wetland resource to store flood water and decrease flooding is reduced. Thus, condition assessment may provide information on the status of ecological services provided by wetlands across the landscape and potential solutions for restoring those services to better meet the needs of the environment and society (Smith et al. 1995).

How Will the NWCA Assess Wetland Quality?

EPA, in collaboration with committed federal, state, tribal and academic experts from across the country, developed standard methods for collecting wetland data and assessing wetland condition for the conterminous United States. Detailed information on the NWCA technical approach can be found in the documents at www.epa.gov/wetlands/survey. In summary, 900 wetland assessment areas were randomly selected from the USFWS S&T plots using a survey design that ensures the sample is representative of wetland resources at national and regional scales (Stevens and Olsen 2004). The S&T plots were used as the base data layer because they are the most consistent and up to date source of wetland status on a national scale. NWCA sites are distributed across seven of the Cowardin et al. (1979) wetland classes characterized in the

---

[1] U.S. Environmental Protection Agency.

S&T Report to facilitate comparison of the findings from both efforts. In addition, some states invested additional resources to supplement the NWCA survey design to provide state-scale reporting of wetland quality. For example, additional NWCA sites were added in North Dakota to allow reporting of wetland quality for the Prairie Pothole region in that State.

The choice of NWCA field methods and indicators was influenced by considerations of timing and resources, such as the need to complete travel and sampling for each site in one day. Once field crews arrive at a site they will sample the wetland attributes as described below.

Vegetation will be characterized by collecting plant data in five 100-m^2 Vegetation Plots systematically placed across the wetland assessment area. Vegetation is a major component of biodiversity found in wetlands and provides habitat for a myriad of organisms. The composition and abundance of plant species is both reflective of, and may influence, the hydrology, water quality, and soil characteristics of a wetland. Plants respond to, and reflect, physical, chemical, or biological disturbances and stressors (Selinger-Looten et al. 1999; Rayamajhi et al. 2006). In addition, the presence and abundance of alien plant species often reflect degraded or declining quality.

Algae data will be collected from sediments (benthic samples), the surface of vegetation stems and leaves (epiphytic samples) and, if present, surface water. Algae respond rapidly to ecological change in wetlands and have been widely used as indicators of wetland condition because of their rapid reproduction rates, short life cycles, and broad distribution (McCormick and Cairns, 1994). More notably, because nutrients such as nitrogen and phosphorus are limiting factors to most types of algae, they respond quickly to excess nutrients. In addition, diatom species can provide insights into past hydrology such as recent flooding, standing water, or droughts (Lane and Brown 2007; USEPA 2002; McCormick and Cairns 1994).

Soils data will be collected in four soil pits and will include an on-site description of the soil profile and collection of three types of soil samples (chemistry,

bulk density, and stable isotope) for laboratory analysis. Soils cycle nutrients, store pollutants, mediate groundwater, and provide habitat for microorganisms, invertebrates, and other more complex organisms (Richardson and Vepraskas, 2001). Biogeochemical processes and ecosystem services that rely on hydric soils or soils with hydric indicators[2] directly influence wetland condition. Soil structure and chemistry can indicate water quality and hydrology (Hargreaves et al., 2003; Mitsch and Gosselink, 2007)[3].

Hydrologic data will include an assessment of hydrologic sources and connectivity, indirect evidence of hydroperiod, estimates of hydrologic fluctuations, and documentation of hydrology alterations or stressors. Wetland hydrology is the primary driver of wetland formation and persistence. Hydrology impacts soil geochemical dynamics, plant productivity, nutrient cycling, and accretion and erosion of organic and inorganic materials in wetlands (Mitsch and Gosselink 2007).

When standing water is present at a wetland assessment area, **water chemistry** samples will be taken and analyzed for general surface water conditions, various chemical analytes, and evidence of disturbance. Total nitrogen and phosphorus reflect the trophic state of the wetland, providing crucial information on possible eutrophication (Keddy 1983). Anthropogenic disturbances such as hydrologic modifications and land use changes are known to alter water quality variables (Lane and Brown, 2007).

The NWCA will also verify the utility across regions and wetland classes of the newly developed **USA Rapid Assessment Method (USA RAM)**. Rapid assessment methods are becoming increasingly useful tools for evaluating the ecological integrity of wetlands and the risk posed by stressors affecting the broader environment. (Fennessy et al. 2007).

---

[2] Not all wetlands occur on listed hydric soils. Small inclusions or wetlands on non-hydric soils units should exhibit hydric indicators. Newly created wetlands on non-hydric soils may lack such indicators.

[3] Some Cowardin et al. wetland types can occur on non-soil substrates such as alluvial deposits, sand or rock.

The primary purpose of USA-RAM is to effectively assess wetland condition in a substantially shorter timeframe than required for more detailed sampling. It unites information gained from field observations of wetland ecology, buffers and stressors. Once verified, USA-RAM will provide States and Tribes with a wetland assessment framework that can be adapted to meet their own monitoring needs.

The NWCA will use a reference-based approach to assess wetland quality nationally and regionally. This involves comparing survey data to assessments of high quality wetlands of similar type and geographic region. The data will be combined and summarized in a variety of ways, with a particular focus on the development of Multi-Metric Indices (MMI). A MMI summarizes various wetland attributes or metrics into one score or index (Karr and Chu 1999). This index is then used to rank the condition of the resource in broad categories. Stressor data will be reported based on how commonly stressors were observed and how severely they impact NWCA sample sites. The final results will not reflect the condition of individual sample sites but instead will be aggregated to describe condition of wetlands by type across the Nation and in regions where a statistically significant number of sites were sampled.

How Will the NWCA Data Be Used?

The 2011 NWCA will provide the baseline for wetland quality in the conterminous United States. Subsequent iterations will be used to track trends in quality by wetland class and region of the country. When paired with the S&T report information, we will for the first time be able to measure progress toward the National goal to increase the quantity and quality of the Nation's wetlands. The S&T Report is an integrated assessment of the net effect of all actions affecting wetland acreage across the nation. Similarly, the NWCA will be an integrated gauge of wetland condition nationwide, summarizing the cumulative effects of federal, state, tribal and local government and private party actions that either degrade wetlands or protect and restore their ecological condition.

Combining the USFWS and EPA data on wetland quantity and quality can potentially be used to inform broad scale environmental goals and priority-setting. For example, the combined data might reveal that estuarine marshes in a region of the country have declining acreage, poor quality, and are often impacted by excess nutrients and buffer fragmentation. This information sets the stage for federal, state or tribal agencies to consider a number of potential actions to counter these trends. They could pursue collaborative partnerships with conservation and water protection programs and stakeholders to leverage resources designated for shoreline restoration or nutrient reduction strategies. Wetland permit data could be examined to determine if certain wetland types are disproportionately impacted and whether mitigation practices are reaching ecological performance standards. In addition, agencies could consider how grant funds are allocated and provide greater incentives for reestablishment and protection activities in estuarine marshes.

As another example, NWCA data may indicate that wetland quality is consistently high in certain regions of the country. The data could be used by agencies to highlight the success of their management framework and encourage continued stewardship into the future. It may lead to consideration of focusing on other wetland types or aquatic resources that may need more attention. Key lessons could be shared with other regions of the country where wetlands were found to be more degraded. Data from high quality wetlands in this region could also be used to establish ecologically-meaningful performance standards for reestablishment and compensatory mitigation projects.

When complete, the 2011 NWCA will represent an influential advancement in the science of wetland monitoring and assessment. The planning process has already succeeded in forging strong partnerships among federal agencies, state agencies, tribes, and non-governmental organizations around the shared goal of improved national data describing wetland quality to support policy and management decisions. In many ways, the NWCA is pushing the limits of our conceptual and technical knowledge by producing a condition assessment at the national scale in one field season. While subsequent national wetland condition surveys will no doubt benefit from the lessons learned during this precedential effort, the 2011 survey will mark a significant leap forward in our understanding of wetlands science and assessment at the national scale.

Figures A and B. Same Wetland Type, Very Different Ecological Condition: The National Wetland Condition Assessment (NWCA) will provide quantitative information on wetlands that have been classified as the same type in Status and Trends but represent considerably different ecological conditions. Figure A is a forested wetland in the middle of a clear cut and re-planted pine plantation in Georgia; Figure B is a virgin cypress forest in Florida. In Status and Trends, both sites would contribute to the national estimates of forested wetland acreage. NWCA would provide more insight into the relative ecological function of each site. The NWCA would likely find that the site in Figure B has high vegetative diversity and vertical complexity, intact soil structure, and healthy amounts of inundation and saturation. Depending on the presence of chemicals in the soil and surface water, the wetland in Figure B would likely have a very high condition assessment. The wetland in Figure A, on the other hand, would likely have very few characteristics of a healthy forested wetland. The vegetative community has been severely disturbed and a considerable number of stressors are evident, including a complete lack of vegetated buffer, extreme soil disturbance, and evidence of recent logging. It is very likely that the Figure A site would be assessed as poor ecological condition for the NWCA.

Acknowledgments

The development of a logistically feasible and scientifically sound technical approach for the NWCA is due to the contributions of many federal, state, tribal and private organizations. The USFWS provided extensive technical support for the survey design and production of site maps. The USDA Natural Resources Conservation Service provided significant technical support for the development of soils field and laboratory protocols. NOAA and National Park Service reviewed the field protocols and provided examples of high quality wetland reference sites. U.S. Geological Survey, Kansas Water Science Center provided significant technical support for the development of field and lab protocols for algal toxins. EPA Scientists from EPA's Office of Research and Development and Regional Offices provided invaluable technical feedback on all components of the NWCA technical approach. The Association of State Wetlands Managers supported the planning process by keeping their membership engaged and aware of the NWCA. Finally, our committed state and tribal partners provided tireless effort in reviewing protocols, attending planning workshops, challenging our thinking, and committing to the goal of improved national data describing wetland quality.

State Wetland Monitoring in Action

Many state wetland managers already use locally-derived wetland quantity and quality information to protect and restore their wetland resources. A particularly strong example is the Nanticoke River Watershed Wetland Restoration Plan from the State of Delaware. Although the Plan makes use of more extensive data than will be produced by the NWCA and S&T, the backbone of this effort is scientifically sound data describing the location, quantity and quality of wetlands and aquatic resources in the watershed. The planning team spent considerable effort creating a comprehensive, digital map of wetlands in the watershed using a variety of data sources, and then randomly-selected a population of wetlands to sample using locally-calibrated wetland assessment methods. Data describing the vegetative community, hydrologic condition, and wetland stressors were analyzed to produce an Index of Wetland Condition and identify the predominant stressors that are degrading wetland quality. Primary stressors were determined for each wetland type and used to develop restoration goals and targets. Based on this analysis the restoration plan identified the following as top conservation targets: 1. Increase and enhance headwater forests/ large forest blocks (which include both uplands and wetlands), 2. Restore channelized streams, and 3. Increase riparian and tidal wetland buffers.

Amy Jacobs, DE DNREC

Potential Vulnerability of Selected Wetland Types to Climatic Changes

The analysis of climate change related impacts to natural resources and the potential responses to those impacts has become a priority for Federal agencies to address (U.S. Department of the Interior 2009). Due in part to their limited capacity for adaptation, wetlands have been considered among the ecosystems most vulnerable to climate change (Bates *et al.* 2008). Because wetlands support a number of trust species and have been linked to water quality and other environmental values, their susceptibility to climatic changes are important to a number of Federal and State agencies.

Direct and indirect environmental changes and related impacts resulting from climatic changes have been recognized and widely accepted by the scientific community (Twilley 2001; Field *et al.* 2007; Nicholls *et al.* 2007). The USEPA (2010e) identified erosion, water quality, salt water intrusion and changes in salinity, species composition and wetland distribution as likely conditions exacerbated by climate and sea level changes. Some of these changes have the potential to influence all wetland types and biota. For example, increases in water temperatures as a result of climate change will alter fundamental ecological processes and the geographic distribution of aquatic species (Poff *et al.* 2002). Similarly, predicted changes in temperature and rainfall will likely reduce habitats vital for waterfowl species and many other wetland birds (NABCI 2010).

Deciphering how and if those changes manifest themselves on the landscape presents challenges for recognizing and following wetland ecosystem adaptations or modifications. This has been further complicated by several factors including decadal or cyclical change, and human induced changes to wetlands and surface waters that mask climate change effects on the landscape (e.g., increased level of farming of drier, shallow wetland basins). In addition, some important changes to species health or distribution may go unrecognized by landscape or land use level survey techniques (e.g., disappearance of cold water fish species from their current geographic range). Recognition of the increased or decreased occurrence and duration of water retention, depth, vegetation patterns, stress responses and community structure may require a refined suite of observables not yet fully understood. There has been acknowledgment that a major challenge of addressing climate change effects on wetlands involves identifying and addressing uncertainty in understanding how that change will affect ecological systems (USFWS 2010).

Wetlands are water dependent and many of the benefits they provide to fish and wildlife species (vegetation for food or cover, nesting and resting habitat, breeding grounds and water) are dependent on precipitation, and other surface and ground water sources. Changes in climatic conditions that affect water conditions (wetter, drier, more saline, etc.) will have a substantial impact on species that utilize wetlands and other ecological services wetlands provide, or make efforts to reestablish wetlands more challenging. Climate change also may influence wetland habitats indirectly such as altered fire regimes, changes in farming techniques and duration, or changes in population concentrations and development patterns.

Researchers have pointed to some types of wetlands that may be particularly vulnerable to the effects of climate change (Guntenspergen *et al.* 2002; Johnson *et al.* 2005; Kirwan *et al.* 2010). Winter (2000) indicated that the wetlands most vulnerable to climate change are those dependent primarily on precipitation for their water supply. These habitats are generally isolated either by lack of hydrological connectivity or by the uniqueness of community assemblage and structure. This makes adjustment to climate change in these areas unlikely and these wetlands face more immediate threats with little chance for adaptation.

In coastal regions such changes may include variations in ocean and air temperatures, acidification, increases or decreases in freshwater runoff (Kling and Sanchirico 2009), changes in species distribution and diversity, erosion of coastal sediments and beaches, inundation of coastal wetlands, increasing salinity of some brackish or freshwater systems and increased storm frequency and intensity. Sea level rise is expected to have a large, sustained impact on future coastal evolution (Beavers 2002) and some of those issues related to saltwater wetlands have been discussed previously (see: *Changes in Sea Level and Coastal Processes Affecting Marine and Estuarine Wetlands*).

The use of geospatially fixed sample areas provide a unique advantage in detecting changes over periodic time intervals and given the limitations cited above, provide information about particular types of wetlands that have exhibited changes in extent or distribution. Table 5 shows the wetland types that most likely exhibited physical change due to climate processes in this study. Other wetlands may have been modified or otherwise affected by climatic factors but were not included based on the geospatial information available.

Small prairie pothole wetland, North Dakota, 2009.

Table 5. Wetland types identified in this study exhibiting change in extent or distribution from climatic conditions.

Wetland Type	*Geographic Extent*	*Observed Changes*	*Supporting Literature Citations*
Marine and Estuarine Systems			
Marine and estuarine tidal shores, sand bars, flats and small barrier islands	South Atlantic Gulf of Mexico	Increasing instability, volatile change or movement, loss of sediment, overwash, translocation	Erwin 2009; Feagin *et al.* 2005; Guntenspergen *et al.* 2002; Thieler and Hammar-Klose 1999
Estuarine forests adjacent to coastlines	Mid and South Atlantic	Shifts in species composition, reduced structural complexity, inundation, chronic salinity stress, disappearance	Riggs and Ames 2003; Rybczyk *et al.* 1995; Stone and Finkl 1995
Mangrove forests (climax community)	Gulf of Mexico	Shifts in species composition, reduced structural complexity, disappearance	Poff *et al.* 2002; Krauss *et al.* 2008; Lugo 1997
Freshwater Systems			
Drier-end emergent depressions including playas of the high plains, vernal pools, small shallow pothole-like depressions and saturated swales[1]	Interior freshwater wetlands of the conterminous United States.	Extended periods of inundation or drought, increased frequency and duration of tillage and farming, sedimentation, disappearance	CA Natural Res. Agency 2010; Matthews 2008; Johnson *et al.* 2005; Poff *et al.* 2002; Whigham 1999
Emergent marshes contiguous with the Great Lakes[2]	Emergent marshes with direct hydrologic connection to the Great Lakes	Extended periods of inundation or drought, transition to different vegetated community types	Webb 2008; Sousounis and Glick 2007; Poff *et al.* 2002; Chao 1999; Magnuson *et al.* 1997

[1] *Small, shallow wetlands are already stressed as ecological transition zones between aquatic and terrestrial ecosystems, making them particularly sensitive to changes in temperature and precipitation. If conditions become warmer and drier these wetlands may become more ephemeral or disappear.*

[2] *The potential for lake-level declines in some of the Great Lakes is projected to exceed the rate of change projected for sea level rise.*

Summary

This study examined recent trends in wetland extent and habitat type throughout the conterminous United States between 2004 and 2009. The study found that recent past trends of reducing wetland losses had been reversed and losses of certain wetland types had increased.

Marine and estuarine wetlands were grouped into three types: estuarine intertidal emergent wetlands (salt and brackish water marshes); estuarine shrub wetlands (mangrove swamps and other salt-tolerant woody species); and estuarine and marine intertidal non-vegetated wetlands. Intertidal marine and estuarine wetland area declined by an estimated 1.4 percent. The largest acreage change was an estimated loss of 111,500 acres (45,140 ha) of estuarine emergent wetland. Losses of estuarine emergent (salt marsh) and changes in marine and estuarine non-vegetated wetlands were attributable to the impacts of coastal storms and relative sea level rise along the coastlines of the Atlantic and Gulf of Mexico. Non-vegetated intertidal wetlands (tidal beaches, shoals, bars and barrier islands) along the Atlantic and the Gulf of Mexico sustained considerable change, increasing by an estimated 2.2 percent in area. These wetlands exhibited marked instability and despite an increase in acreage, are most likely to sustain additional physical changes from ongoing and future coastal events. There has been growing awareness of the threats posed to coastal environments as a variety of stressors interact with climate-related processes, potentially increasing the vulnerability of these coastal wetland areas to change.

Freshwater wetland types had an estimated net gain in area of 21,900 acres (8,900 ha). This was largely supported by increased area in freshwater ponds. Freshwater vegetated wetlands continued a long-term trend and declined by 0.2 percent in area although this rate of loss was reduced by 50 percent from the previous era. Overall freshwater wetland losses have continued particularly in regions of the country where there has been potential for wetlands to come into conflict with competing land and resource development interests. Questions remain regarding the status of freshwater wetlands that may no longer be subject to Federal protection as a result of legal decisions or changes in regulatory policy, as forested wetlands sustained their largest losses since the 1974 to 1985 time period.

Freshwater ponds have continued to increase and the additional categorization of freshwater pond types provided information on these trends, as well as the distribution and types of open water wetlands on the landscape.

The cumulative effects of losses in the freshwater system have had consequences for hydrologic and ecosystem connectivity in certain regions. Profound reductions in wetland extent have resulted in habitat loss and fragmentation, and may have limited the opportunities for wetland reestablishment and watershed rehabilitation.

There have been a number of successes in conservation, protection and reestablishment of wetlands. Between 2004 and 2009, an estimated 489,600 acres (198,230 ha) of upland were reestablished as wetland. Actions on agriculture lands and "other" lands with undetermined land use were attributed with these gains. Other wetland enhancement projects that did not increase acreage but sought to improve quality were not assessed as part of this study.

Because wetland acreage losses outpaced gains, mitigation, reestablishment or creation of wetlands has not been "in-kind" to replace wetland type or area. Wetland characteristics have shifted from forest and marsh to open water depressions where hydrology is more easily engineered and stabilized. Financial considerations and engineering constraints have likely influenced wetland reestablishment programs to target projects on agricultural lands thus affecting wetland distribution and reestablished wetland type(s).

Because wetland abundance and distribution affect wetland biodiversity, reestablishment and mitigation actions could improve ecological interactions if wetland type (diversity) and geospatial interspersion were considerations. As an initial step, tracking wetland type and geo-position remains an important component for monitoring wetland reestablishment, creation and mitigation projects.

This study recognized that some wetland types have exhibited changes in extent or distribution related to climate-induced changes and while all wetlands exemplify complex interactions between hydrology and climate some areas may be subjected to additional stressors. Changes in climate may affect a much broader group of wetlands by altering temperature, precipitation rates or hydrology but recognizing the outcome of these changes has been complicated by human activities, past hydrological alterations or impacts to larger landscape-level systems. As a result of past actions, fragmented wetland habitats are likely to have less structural stability to withstand either anthropogenic or climatic changes in the future, and failure to restore wetland hydrology and biological integrity may have long-term ecological and economic impacts as reestablishment or mitigation options become more limited.

References Cited

Adams, L.W., L.E. Dove, and T.M. Franklin. 1985. Mallard pair and brood use of urban storm-water control impoundments. Wildlife Society Bulletin, 13:46-51.

Adamus, P.R. 2005. Science Review and Data Analysis for Tidal Wetlands of the Oregon Coast. Part 2 of a Hydrogeomorphic Guidebook. Report to Coos Watershed Association, U.S. Environmental Protection Agency, and Oregon Dept. of State Lands, Salem. 216 p.

Allen, A.W., Y.K. Bernal, and R.J. Moulton. 1996. Pine plantations and wildlife in the Southeastern United States: An assessment of impacts and opportunities. Technical Report 3. U.S. Department of the Interior, National Biological Service, Washington, D.C. 32 p.

Anderson, J.R., E.E. Hardy, J.T. Roach, and R.E. Winter. 1976. A land use and land cover classification system for use with remote sensor data. U.S. Geological Survey Professional Paper 964. U.S. Geological Survey, Washington, D.C. 28 p.

Baldassarre, G.A. and E.G. Bolen. 1994. Waterfowl Ecology and Management. John Wiley and Sons, Inc. 609 p.

Barber, L.B., S.H. Keefe, R.C. Antweiler, H.E. Taylor, and R.D. Wass. 2006. Accumulation of Contaminants in Fish from Wastewater Treatment Wetlands. Environmental Science and Technology, Vol. 40, No. 2. pp. 603-611.

Bates, B.C., Z.W. Kundzewicz, S. Wu, and J.P. Palutikof (eds.). 2008. Climate Change and Water. Technical Paper of the Intergovernmental Panel on Climate Change, IPCC Secretariat, Geneva, 210 p.

Batzer, D.P. and R.R. Sharitz (eds.). 2006. Ecology of Freshwater and Estuarine Wetlands. Univ. of CA Press, Berkeley. 568 p.

Beauchamp, S.K. 1996. Cypress: From wetlands and wildlife habitat to flowerbeds and front yards. University of Florida, Institute of Food and Agricultural Sciences, Gainesville, FL.

Bedford, B.L. 1996. The need to define hydrologic equivalence at the landscape scale for freshwater wetlands mitigation. Ecological Applications, Vol. 6, No. 1. pp. 57-68.

Bedford, B.L. 1999. Cumulative effects on wetland landscapes: Links to wetland restoration in the United States and Southern Canada. Wetlands, Vol. 19, No. 4. pp. 775-788.

Bedford, B.L. and E.M. Preston. 1988. Developing the scientific basis for assessing cumulative effects of wetland loss and degradation on landscape functions: Status, perspectives, and prospects. Environmental Management, Vol. 12, No. 5. pp. 751-771.

Beavers, R. 2002. Vulnerability of U.S. National Parks to sea-level rise and coastal change. National Park Service, Natural Resource Program Center, Geologic Resources Division, Denver, CO. USGS Fact Sheet FS–095–02.

Biebighauser, T.R. 2007. Wetland Drainage, Restoration, and Repair. The University Press of Kentucky, Lexington, KY. 241 p.

Blann, K.L., J.L. Anderson, G.R. Sands, and B. Vondracek. 2009. Effects of Agricultural Drainage on Aquatic Ecosystems: A Review. Critical Reviews in Environmental Science and Technology, 39. pp. 909–1001.

Bliss, C. and N.B. Comerford. 2002. Influence of forest harvesting on water table dynamics in a Florida flatwoods landscape. Journal of Soil Society of America, 66:1344-1349.

Brooks, R.P., D.H. Wardrop, C.A. Cole, and D.A. Campbell. 2005. Are we purveyors of wetland homogeneity? A model of degradation and restoration to improve wetland mitigation performance. In: W. J. Mitsch (ed.). Wetland Creation, Restoration and Conservation – the State of the Science. Elsevier, Amsterdam. pp. 331-340.

California Natural Resources Agency. 2010. State of the State's wetlands – 10 years if challenges and progress. On-line resource: http://www.californiawetlands.net/static/documents/Final_SOSW_Report_09232010.pdf

Cain, M.J. 2008. Wisconsin's Wetland Regulatory Program. Wisconsin Department of Natural Resources, Madison, WI. 12 p.

Capel, S., B. Carmichael, M. Gudlin, and D. Long. 1995. Wildlife habitat needs assessment, Southeast region. Transactions North American Wildlife and Natural Resources Conference, 60:288-299.

Casey, R.A. and S.J. Klaine. 2001. Nutrient attenuation by a riparian wetland during natural and artificial runoff events. Journal of Environmental Quality, 30:1720–1731.

Chao, P.T. 1999. Great Lakes Water Resources–Climate Change Impact Analysis. In: Proc. Specialty Conf. on Potential Consequences of Climate Variability and Change to Water Resources of the United States, American Water Resources Assoc., Atlanta, GA. pp. 307-310.

Chertok, M.A. and K. Sinding. 2005. Federal jurisdiction over wetlands: "Waters of the United States". In: K.D. Connolly, S.M. Johnson and D.R. Williams, Wetlands Law and Policy - understanding Section 404. Section of Environment, Energy, and Resources. American Bar Association. pp. 59-104.

Copeland, C. 2010. Wetlands: An overview of issues. Congressional Research Service, 7-5700, RL33483. 22 p.

Corbett, D.R., J.P. Walsh, L. Cowart, S.R. Riggs, D.V. Ames, and S.J. Culver. 2008. Shoreline change within the Albemarle-Pamlico estuarine system, North Carolina. Department of Geological Sciences, Thomas Harriot College of Arts and Sciences and Institute for Coastal Science and Policy, East Carolina University, Greenville, NC. 10 p.

Costanza, R., O. Perez-Maqueo, M.L. Martinez, P. Sutton, S.J. Anderson, and K. Mulder. 2008. The value of coastal wetlands for hurricane protection. Ambio. Vol. 37, No. 4, pp. 241-248.

Council on Environmental Quality. 2008. Conserving America's wetlands. The White House Council on Environmental Quality, Washington, D.C. 57 p.

Council on Environmental Quality. 2009. Letter to Senator Barbara Boxer, Chair Committee on Environment and Public Works. The White House Council on Environmental Quality, Washington, D.C.

Cowardin, L.M. and F.C. Golet. 1995. US Fish and Wildlife Service 1979 wetland classification: A review. Vegetatio 118. pp. 139-152.

Cowardin, L.M, V. Carter, F.C. Golet, and E.T. LaRoe. 1979. Classification of wetlands and deepwater habitats of the United States. Department of the Interior. U.S. Fish and Wildlife Service, Washington, D.C. 131 p.

Craighead, F.C. 1971. The trees of south Florida. University of Miami Press, Coral Gables, FL.

Dahl, T.E. 2000. Status and trends of wetlands in the conterminous United States 1986 to 1997. U.S. Department of the Interior, Fish and Wildlife Service, Washington, D.C. 82 p.

Dahl, T.E. 2004. Remote sensing as a tool for monitoring wetland habitat change. In: Aguirre-Bravo, Celedonio, and others. eds. 2004. Monitoring Science and Technology Symposium: Unifying knowledge for sustainability in the Western Hemisphere; 2004 September 20-24; Denver, CO. Proceedings RMRS-P-000. Ogden, UT: U.S. Department of Agriculture, Forest Service, Rocky Mountain Research Station.

Dahl, T.E. 2005. Florida's Wetlands–An Update on Status and Trends 1985 to 1996. U.S. Department of Interior, Fish and Wildlife Service, Washington, D.C. 80 p.

Dahl, T.E. 2006. Status and trends of wetlands in the conterminous United States 1998 to 2004. U.S. Department of the Interior, Fish and Wildlife Service, Washington, D.C. 112 p.

Dahl, T.E. In manuscript. Survey design and spatial sampling techniques to monitor wetland area and change in the United States. U.S. Fish and Wildlife Service.

Dahl, T.E. and G.J. Allord. 1996. History of wetlands in the conterminous United States. In. J. D. Fretwell, J.S. Williams, and P. J. Redman (compilers) National Water Summary on Wetland Resources. U.S. Geological Survey Water-Supply Paper 2425. pp. 19-26.

Dahl, T.E. and M.T. Bergeson. 2009. Technical procedures for conducting status and trends of the Nation's wetlands. U.S. Fish and Wildlife Service, Division of Habitat and Resource Conservation, Washington, D.C. 74 p.

Dahl, T.E. and C.E. Johnson. 1991. Status and trends of wetlands in the conterminous United States, mid-1970s to mid-1980s. U.S. Department of the Interior. U.S. Fish and Wildlife Service, Washington, D.C. 28 p.

Dahl, T.E. and M.D. Watmough. 2007. Current approaches to wetland status and trends monitoring in prairie Canada and the continental United States of America. Canadian Journal of Remote Sensing, Vol. 33, Suppl. 1. pp. S17–S27.

Dahl, T.E., J. Swords, and M.T. Bergeson. 2009. Wetland inventory of the Yazoo Backwater Area, Mississippi—Wetland status and potential changes based on an updated inventory using remotely sensed imagery. U.S. Fish and Wildlife Service, Division of Habitat and Resource Conservation, Washington, D.C. 30 p.

Davis, B.E. and A.D. Afton. 2010. Movement distances and habitat switching by female mallards wintering in the Lower Mississippi Alluvial Valley. Waterbirds, Vol. 33, No. 3. pp. 349-356.

Day, J.W., R.R. Christian, D.M. Boesch, A. Yanez-Arancibia, J. Morris, R.R. Twilley, L. Naylor, L. Schaffner, and C. Stevenson. 2008. Consequences of climate change on the Ecogeomorphology of coastal wetlands. Estuaries and Coasts. 31:477-491.

Dechka. J.A., S.E. Franklin, M.D. Watmough, R.P. Bennett, and D.W. Ingstrup. 2002. Classification of wetland habitat and vegetation communities using multi-temporal Ikonos imagery in southern Saskatchewan. Can. J. Remote Sensing, Vol. 28. No. 5. pp. 679-685.

deMaynadier, P.G. and M.L. Hunter, Jr. 1995. The relationship between forest management and amphibian ecology: A review of the North American literature. Environ. Rev. 3:230-261.

De Steven, D. 2009. Interim Report: Assessing wetlands restoration and creation practices implemented under U.S. Department of Agriculture conservation programs in the southeastern coastal plain. U.S. Forest Service Southern Research Station, Center for Bottomland Hardwoods Research, Stoneville, MS. 7 p.

Dierssen, H.M., R.C. Zimmerman, R.A. Leathers, T.V. Downes, and C.O. Davis. 2003. Ocean color remote sensing of seagrass and bathymetry in the Bahamas Bank by high-resolution airborne imagery. Limnology and Oceanography, Vol. 48, No. 1. part 2. pp. 444-455.

Dokka, R.K. 2006. Modern-day tectonic subsidence in coastal Louisiana. Geology, Vol. 34, No. 4. pp. 281-284.

Doss, C.R. and S.J. Taff. 1996. The influence of wetland type and wetland proximity on residential property values. Journal of Agricultural and Resource Economics. 21(1). pp. 120-129.

Downing, D.M., C Winer and L.D. Wood. 2003. Navigating through Clean Water Act jurisdiction: A legal review. Wetlands, Vol.23, No.3. pp. 475-493.

Doyle, T.W. 1997. Modeling hurricane effects on mangrove ecosystems. Department of the Interior, U.S. Geological Survey, Fact Sheet 095-97.

Ducks Unlimited. 2009. Updating the National Wetlands Inventory for Ohio–Final Report. Ducks Unlimited, Inc., Great Lakes/ Atlantic Regional Office, Ann Arbor, MI. 119 p.

Erwin, K.L. 2009. Wetlands and global climate change: the role of wetland restoration in a changing world. Wetlands Ecology and Management. Vol. 17. pp. 71–84.

Euliss, N.H. Jr., L.M. Smith, D.A. Wilcox, and B.A. Browne. 2008. Linking ecosystem processes with wetland management goals: Charting a course for a sustainable future. Wetlands, 28(3): 553-562.

Feagin, R.A., D.J. Sherman, and W.E. Grant. 2005. Coastal erosion, global sea-level rise, and the loss of sand dune plant habitats. Front. Ecol. Environ. Vol. 3, No. 7. pp. 359–364.

Federal Geographic Data Committee. 1996. On-line resource: http:// www.fgdc.gov/standards/projects/ FGDC-standards-projects/ wetlands/?searchterm=wetlands.

Fennessy, M.S., A.D. Jacobs, and M.E. Kentula. 2004. Review of rapid methods for assessing wetland condition. EPA-620-R-04_009. U.S. Environmental Protection Agency, Washington, D.C.

Fennessy, M.S., A.D. Jacobs, and M.E. Kentula. 2007. An evaluation of rapid methods for assessing the ecological condition of wetlands. Wetlands. 27(3):543-560.

Field, C.B., L.D. Mortsch, M. Braklacich, D.L. Forbes, P. Kovacs, J.A. Patz, S.W. Running, and M.J. Scott. 2007. North America In: M.L. Parry, O.F. Canziani, J.P. Palutikof, P.J. van der Linden, and C.E. Hanson, eds. Climate change 2007—impacts, adaptation and vulnerability. Contribution of Working Group II to the Fourth Assessment Report of the Intergovernmental Panel on Climate Change: Cambridge, U.K., and New York, Cambridge University Press. pp. 617–652.

FitzGerald, D.M., Fenster, M.S., Argow, B.A., and Buynevich, I.V. 2008. Coastal impacts due to sea-level rise: Annual Review of Earth and Planetary Sciences, Vol. 36. pp. 601–647.

Florida Department of Agriculture and Consumer Services. 2009. On-line resource: http://www.doacs.state. fl.us/press/2009/01222009.html.

Florida Department of Environmental Protection. 2008. Beach erosion control program. http://www.dep. state.fl.us/beaches/programs/ bcherosn.htm.

Frayer, W.E., T.J. Monahan, D.C. Bowden, and F.A. Graybill. 1983. Status and trends of wetlands and deepwater habitats in the conterminous United States, 1950's to 1970's. Colorado State University, Fort Collins, CO. 31 p.

Frohn, R.C., M. Reif, C. Lane, and B. Autrey. 2009. Satellite remote sensing of isolated wetlands using object-oriented classification of Landsat-7 data. Wetlands. Vol. 29, No. 3. pp. 931-941.

Food and Agriculture Organization of the United Nations. 2007. The world's mangroves 1980-2005. FAO Forestry Paper 153, Rome, Italy. 77 p.

Galloway, D., D.R. Jones, and S.E. Ingebritsen. eds. 1999. Land Subsidence in the United States. U.S. Geological Survey, Circular 1182, Washington, D.C. 177 pp. http://pubs.usgs.gov/circ/circ1182/.

Gardiner, E.S. and J.M. Oliver. 2005. Restoration of bottomland hardwood forests in Lower Mississippi Alluvial Valley, U.S.A. In: J.A. Stanturf and P. Madsen. eds. Restoration of Boreal and Temperate Forests. CRC Press, Boca Raton, FL. pp. 235-251.

Government Accountability Office. 2007. Coastal wetlands: Lessons learned from past efforts in Louisiana could help guide future restoration and protection. GAO-08-130.

Guntenspergen, G.R., B.A. Vairin, and V. Burkett. 2002. Overview of Coastal Wetland Global Climate Change Research. Biological Science Report USGS-BRD-ISBR 1998-2002. U.S. Geological Survey, Lafayette, Louisiana.

Gorham, E. and L. Rochefort. 2003. Peatland restoration: A brief assessment with special reference to Sphagnum bogs. Wetlands Ecology and Management Vol. 11. pp. 109–119.

Hammond, E.H. 1970. Physical subdivisions of the United States of America. In: U.S. Geological Survey. National Atlas of the United States of America. Department of the Interior, Washington, D.C. 61 p.

Hanemann, M., L. Pendleton, C. Mohn, J. Hilger, K. Kurisawa, D. Layton, and F. Vasquez. 2003. Interim report on the southern California beach valuation project. Prepared for the National Ocean and Atmospheric Administration, Minerals Management Service (Department of the Interior), The California State Water Resources Control Board, and The California Department of Fish and Game.

Hargreaves, P.R., P.C. Brookes, G.J. S. Ross, and P.R. Poulton. 2003. Evaluating soil microbial biomass carbon as an indicator of long-term environmental change. Soil Biology and Biochemistry 35:401-407.

Harms, W.R., W.M. Aust, and J.A. Burger. 1998. Wet flatwoods. In: M.G. Messina and W.H Conner. eds. Southern Forested Wetlands: Ecology and Management. CRC Press, Boca Raton, FL. pp. 421-444.

Harrington, B.R. 2008. Coastal inlets as strategic habitat for shorebirds in the southeastern United States. ERDC TN-DOER-E25. U.S. Army Engineering Research and Development Center, Vicksburg, MS. 8 p. http://el.erdc.usace.army. mil/dots/doer/.

Harrington, B.R. and J. Corven. No Date. Shorebird migration – Fundamentals for land managers in the United States. DU # Q0433, Ducks Unlimited, Inc. Memphis, TN. 44 p.

Harris, L.D. and J.G. Gosselink. 1990. Cumulative impacts of bottomland hardwood forest conversion on hydrology, water quality, and terrestrial wildlife. In: Ecological Processes and Cumulative Impacts, J.G Gosselink, L.C. Lee and T.A. Muir. eds. Lewis Publishers, Chelsea, MI. pp. 259-322.

Hasse, J. 2007. Using remote sensing and GIS integration to identify spatial characteristics of sprawl at the building unit level. In: V. Mesev. ed. Integration of GIS and Remote Sensing, John Wiley and Sons, Ltd. pp. 117-147.

Heartland. 2008. State of the catfish industry and Heartland shortages. Letter from Heartland Catfish to brokers and customers. On-line resource: http://www.benekeithfoodservice.com/images/Oklahoma/Second%20Email%20032808/Catfish.pdf.

Heitmeyer, M.E., L.H. Fredrickson, and G.F. Krause. 1989. Water and habitat dynamics of the Mingo Swamp in Southeastern Missouri. Fish Wildl. Res. 6, U.S. Fish and Wildlife Service, Washington, D.C. 26 p.

Jackson, C.R. 2006. Wetland hydrology. In: D.P. Batzer and R.R. Sharitz. eds. Ecology of Freshwater and Estuarine Wetlands. Univ. of CA Press, Berkeley. pp. 43-81.

Jenson, J.R. 2007. Remote sensing of the environment: an earth resource perspective 2nd ed. Pearson Prentice Hall Inc. 592 p.

Johnson, W.C., B.V. Millett, T. Gilmanov, R.A. Voldseth, G.R. Guntenspergen, and D.E. Naugle. 2005. Vulnerability of northern prairie wetlands to climate change. BioScience. 55:863-872.

Karr, J.R., and E.W. Chu. 1999. Restoring life in running waters: Better biological monitoring. Washington, D.C., Island Press.

Keddy, P.A. 1983. Freshwater wetland human-induced changes: indirect effects must also be considered. Environmental Management. 7:299-302.

Kennamer, R.A., J.R. Stout, R.P. Jackson, S.V. Colwell, I.L. Brisbin, and J. Burger. 2005. Mercury patterns in wood duck eggs form a contaminated reservoir in South Carolina, USA. Environmental Toxicology and Chemistry, Vol. 24, No. 7, pp. 1793–1800.

Kentula, M.E. 1996. Wetland restoration and creation. In: J.D. Fretwell, J.S. Williams and P.J. Redman (compilers). National Water Summary on Wetland Resources. U.S. Geological Survey Water-Supply Paper 2425. pp. 87-92.

Kentula, M.E., R.P. Brooks, S.E. Gwin, C.C. Holland, A.D. Sherman, and J.C. Sifneos. 1992. An approach to improving decision making in wetland restoration and creation. Island Press, Washington, D.C. 151 p.

Kentula, M.E., S.E. Gwin, and S.M. Pierson. 2004. Tracking changes in wetlands with urbanization: sixteen years of experience in Portland, Oregon, USA. Wetlands. 24(4):734-743.

Kirwan, M.L., G.R. Guntenspergen, A. D'Alpaos, J.T. Morris, S.M. Mudd, and S. Temmerman. 2010. Limits on the adaptability of coastal marshes to rising sea level. Geophysical Research Letters, Vol. 37, L23401, doi:10.1029. 5 pp.

Kling, D. and J.N. Sanchirico. 2009. An adaptation portfolio for the United States coastal and marine environment. An initiative of the climate policy program, Resources for the Future. 70 p.

Krauss, K.W., C.E. Lovelock, K.L. McKee, L. Lopez-Hoffman, S.M. Ewe, and W.P. Sousa. 2008. Environmental drivers in mangrove establishment and early development: A review. Aquatic Botany. 89(2):105-127.

Kudray, G.M. and T. Schemm. 2008. Wetlands of the Bitterroot Valley: Change and ecological functions. Report to the Montana Department of Environmental Quality. Montana Natural Heritage Program, Helena, Montana. 32 p. plus appendices.

Lane, C.R. and M.T. Brown. 2007. Diatoms as indicators of isolated herbaceous wetland condition in Florida, USA. Ecological Indicators. 7(3):521-540.

Langbein, W.B. and K.T. Iseri. 1960. General introduction and hydrologic definitions manual of hydrology. Part 1. General surface water techniques. U.S. Geological Survey, Water Supply Paper 1541–A. 29 p.

Lavoie, D., ed. 2009. Sand resources, regional geology, and coastal processes of the Chandeleur Islands coastal system—an evaluation of the Breton National Wildlife Refuge: U.S. Geological Survey Scientific Investigations Report 2009–5252, 180 p.

Lichvar, R.W. and J.T. Kartesz. 2009. North American Digital Flora: National Wetland Plant List, version 2.1.0 (https://wetland_plants.usace.army.mil). U.S. Army Corps of Engineers, Engineer Research and Development Center, Cold Regions Research and Engineering Laboratory, Hanover, NH, and BONAP, Chapel Hill, NC.

Lillesand, T.M. and R.W. Kieffer. 1987. Remote Sensing and Image Interpretation 2nd edition. John Wiley and Sons, N.Y. 721 p.

Liudahl, K., D.J. Belz, L. Carey, R.W. Drew, S. Fisher, and R. Pate. 1989. Soil Survey of Collier County Area, Florida. U.S. Department of Agriculture, Natural Resources Conservation Service. 152 p.

Lokemoen, J.T. 1982. Waterfowl production on stock-watering ponds in the northern plains. In: J.T. Ratti, L.D. Flake, and W. Alan Wentz (compilers). Waterfowl Ecology and management: Selected Readings. Wildlife Society, pp. 201-211.

Lu, J., G. Sun, S.G. McNulty, and N.B. Comerford. 2009. Sensitivity of pine flatwoods hydrology to climate change and forest management in Florida, USA. Wetlands, Vol. 29, No. 3. pp. 826–836.

Lugo, A.E. 1997. Old-growth mangrove forests in the United States. Conservation Biology, Vol. 11, No. 1. pp. 11-20.

Matthews, J.H. 2008. Anthropogenic Climate Change in the Playa Lakes Joint Venture Region, Understanding Impacts, Discerning Trends, and Developing Responses. A report prepared for the Playa Lakes Joint Venture. 40 p.

McCormick, P. and J. Cairns. 1994. Algae as indicators of environmental change. Journal of Applied Phycology. 6:509-526.

McCoy, R.M. 2005. Field Methods in Remote Sensing. Guilford Press, New York, NY. 158 p.

Miller, D. 2008. Busting the CRP. Progressive Farmer. Vol. 123, No. 5. pp. 44-48.

Miller, J.A. and J. Rogan. 2007. Using GIS and remote sensing for ecological mapping and monitoring. In: V. Mesev. Integration of GIS and Remote Sensing. John Wiley and Sons, Ltd. pp. 233-268.

Miller, J.H., B.R. Zutter, R.A. Newbold, M.B. Edwards, and S.M. Shepard. 2003. Stand dynamics and plant associates of loblolly pine plantation to mid-rotation after early intensive vegetation management—A southeastern United States regional study. Southern Journal of Applied Forestry, Vol. 27, No. 4. pp. 1-16.

Mitsch, W.J. and J.G. Gosselink. 1993. Wetlands, 2nd ed. Van Nostrand Reinhold, New York. 539 p.

Mitsch, W.J. and J.G. Gosselink. 2007. Wetlands, 4th ed. John Wiley & Sons, Hoboken, N.J. 582 p.

Mitsch, W.J. and R.F. Wilson. 1996. Improving the success of wetland creation and restoration with know-how, time, and self design. Ecological Applications. 6:77-83.

Morton, R.A. and T.L. Miller. 2005. National assessment of shoreline change: Part 2: Historical shoreline changes and associated coastal land loss along the U.S. Southeast Coast. U.S. Geological Survey. Reston, VA.

Morton, R.A., G. Tiling, and N.F. Ferina. 2003. Causes of hot-spot wetland loss in the Mississippi delta plain. Environmental Geosciences. 10:71-80.

National Academy of Sciences. 2008. Ecological impacts of climate change. Committee on Ecological Impacts of Climate Change, The National Academies. Washington, D.C.

National Park Service. 2010. Ecosystems: Mangrove. On-line resource: http://www.nps.gov/ever/naturescience/mangroves.htm.

National Research Council. 1995. Wetlands: Characteristics and boundaries. Committee on Characterization of Wetlands, Water Science and Technology Board. National Academy Press, Washington, D.C. 268 p.

Natural Resources Conservation Service. 2010. National Hydric Soils List by State. On-line resource: http://soils.usda.gov/use/hydric/lists/state.html.

Nicholls, R.J., P.P. Wong, V.R. Burkett, J.O. Codignotto, J.E. Hay, R.F. McLean, S. Ragoonaden, and C.D. Woodroffe. 2007. Coastal systems and low-lying areas. Climate Change 2007: Impacts, Adaptation and Vulnerability. Contribution of Working Group II to the Fourth Assessment Report of the Intergovernmental Panel on Climate Change, M.L. Parry, O.F. Canziani, J.P. Palutikof, P.J. van der Linden and C.E. Hanson, eds., Cambridge University Press, Cambridge, UK. pp. 315-356.

NOAA Congressional Budget Hearing. 2009. Sea Level Rise, Inundation and Storm Surge. Post-Hearing Questions for the Record, Dr. Jane Lubchenco, Administrator, National Oceanic and Atmospheric Administration. FY 2010 NOAA Budget Hearing.

North American Bird Conservation Initiative, U.S. Committee. 2010. The State of the Birds 2010 Report on Climate Change, United States of America. U.S. Department of the Interior: Washington, DC.

North Carolina State University. 2008. Major causes of wetland loss and degradation. On-line resource: http://www.water.ncsu.edu/watershedss/info/wetlands/wetloss.html.

North Dakota Game and Fish Department. 2008. On-line resource: http://www.ppjv.org/PPJV_presntations/CRP_RIP_June_2008.pdf.

Oertli, B., J. Biggs, R. Cereghino, P. Grillas, P. Joly, and J. Lachavanne. 2005. Conservation and monitoring of pond biodiversity. Aquatic Conservation: Marine and Freshwater Ecosystems. 15:535-540.

Oertli, B., D.A. Joye, E. Castella, R. Juge, D. Cambin, and J.B. Lachavanne. 2002. Does size matter? The relationship between pond area and biodiversity. Biological Conservation, 104. pp. 59-70.

Olsen, A.R., J. Sedransk, D. Edwards, C.A. Gotway, W. Liggett, S. Rathbun, K.H. Reckhow, and L.J. Young. 1999. Statistical issues for monitoring ecological and natural resources in the United States. Environmental Monitoring and Assessment. 54:1-45.

Patience, N. and V. Klemas. 1993. Wetland Functional health assessment using remote sensing and other techniques: Literature search. U.S. Department of Commerce, National Oceanic and Atmospheric Administration, National Marine Fisheries Service, SE Fisheries Science Center, Beaufort Laboratory, Beaufort, NC. 60 p.

Peneva, E., J.A. Griffith and G.A. Carter. 2008. Seagrass mapping in the northern Gulf of Mexico using airborne hyperspectral imagery: A comparison of classification methods. Journal of Coastal Research. Vol. 24, No. 4, pp. 850-856.

Phillips, G. 2008. Farm-raised catfish: Challenging times. Mississippi Farm Country. A Publication of Mississippi Farm Bureau Federation. Vol. 84, No. 5. pp. 8-12.

Philipson, W. ed. 1996. Manual of Photographic Interpretation (Second edition). American Society for Photogrammetry and Remote Sensing. Bethesda, MD.

Poff, N.L., M.M. Brinson, and J.W. Day, Jr. 2002. Aquatic ecosystems and global climate change: Potential impacts on inland freshwater and coastal wetland ecosystems in the United States. Pew Center on Global Climate Change. 44 p.

Rayamajhi, M., T. Van, P. Pratt, and T. Center. 2006. Temporal and structural effects of stands on litter production in the Melalueca quinquenervia dominated wetlands of south Florida. Wetlands Ecology and Management. 14:303-316.

Richardson, J.L. and M.J. Vepraskas. 2001. Wetland Soils: Genesis, Hydrology, Landscape, and Classification. Lewis Publishers, Boca Raton, Florida, USA.

Riggs, S.R. and D.V. Ame. 2003. Drowning the North Carolina Coast: Sea-level rise and estuarine dynamics. North Carolina Department of Environment and Natural Resources, Division of Coastal Management and North Carolina Sea Grant, North Carolina State University, Raleigh, NC. 152 p.

Rogan, J., J. Franklin, and D.A. Roberts. 2002. A comparison of methods for monitoring multitemporal vegetation change using Thematic Mapper imagery. Remote Sensing of Environment. 80. pp. 143-156.

Roghair, L.D. 2009. Pilot Study Sample data Transfer to Contributed Restored Wetlands Geodatabase. Conservation Management Institute, Virginia Polytechnic Institute and State University, Blacksburg, VA. 30 p.

Ruffolo, J. 2002. The U.S. Supreme Court limits federal regulation of wetlands: Implications of the SWANCC Decision. California Research Bureau, CRB 02-003, Sacramento, CA. 129 p.

Ruwaldt, J.J. Jr., L.D. Flake, and J.M. Gates. 1979. Waterfowl pair use of natural and man-made wetlands in South Dakota. J. Wildlife Management. 43(2): 375-383.

Rybczyk, J.M., X. Zhang, J. Day, I. Heese, and S. Feagley. 1995. The impact of Hurricane Andrew on tree mortality, litterfall, nutrient flux, and water quality in a Louisiana coastal swamp forest. Journal of Coastal Research, 21, pp. 340–353.

Sanders, B.F. and F. Arega. 2002. Hydrodynamic design in coastal wetland restoration. California Water Resources Center, University of CA, Irvine. Technical Completion Report - Project UCAL-WRC-W-942. 15 p.

Sarndal, C.E., B. Swensson, and J. Wretman. 1992. Model assisted survey sampling. Springer-Verlag, New York, NY.

Schoenholtz, S.H., J.P. James, R.M. Kaminski, B.D. Leopold, and A.W. Ezell. 2001. Afforestation of bottomland hardwoods in the Lower Mississippi Alluvial Valley: Status and trends. Wetlands, Vol. 21, No. 4. pp. 602–613.

Selinger-Looten, R., F. Grevilliot, and S. Muller. 1999. Structure of plant communities and landscape patterns in alluvial meadows of two flooded plains in the north-east of France. Landscape Ecology. 14:213-229.

Sharitz R.R. and C.A. Gresham. 1998. Pocosins and Carolina Bays. In: M. G. Messina and W. H. Conner. Southern Forested Wetlands: Ecology and Management. Lewis Publishers. Boca Raton, FL, USA.

Simenstad, C.A., W.G. Hood, R.M. Thom, D.A. Levy, and D.L. Bottom. 2002. Landscape structure and scale constraints on restoring estuarine wetlands for Pacific Coast juvenile fishes. Concepts and Controversies in Tidal Marsh Ecology, Part 7, DOI: 10.1007/0-306-47534-0_28. pp. 597-630.

Showalter, S. and S. Spigener. 2008. University of Mississippi. Mississippi—Alabama Sea Grant Legal Program, Oxford, MS. On-line resource: http://www.olemiss.edu/orgs/SGLC/MSAL/Water%20Log/28.1yazoo.html.

Smith, T.J. III. 2004. Development of a long-term sampling network to monitor restoration success in the Southwest coastal Everglades: vegetation, hydrology, and sediments. U.S. Geological Survey, Fact Sheet 2004-3015. http://sofia.usgs.gov/publications/fs/2004-3015.

Smith, R.D., A. Ammann, C. Bartoldus, and M.M. Brinson. 1995. An approach for assessing wetland function using hydrogeomorphic classification, reference wetlands, and functional indices. Waterways Experiment Stations, U.S. Army Corps of Engineers, Vicksburg, MS, USA, Technical Report WRP-DE-9.

Smith, C.G., S.J. Culver, S.R. Riggs, D. Ames, D.R. Corbett and D. Mallinson. 2008. Geospatial analysis of barrier island width of two segments of the Outer Banks, North Carolina, USA: Anthropogenic curtailment of natural self-sustaining processes. Journal of Coastal Research, 24:1. pp. 70-83.

Smith, W.B., P.D. Miles, C.H. Perry, and S.A. Pugh. 2009. Forest Resources of the United States, 2007. Gen. Tech. Rep. WO-78. Washington, DC: U.S. Department of Agriculture, Forest Service, Washington Office. 336 p.

Sousounis, P. and P. Glick. 2007. The Potential Impacts of Global Warming on the Great Lakes Region. On-line resource: www.climatehotmap.org/impacts/greatlakes.html.

Stedman, S.M. and T.E. Dahl. 2008. Status and trends of wetlands in the coastal watersheds of the Eastern United States 1998 to 2004. National Oceanic and Atmospheric Administration, National Marine Fisheries Service and U.S. Department of the Interior, Fish and Wildlife Service. 32 p.

Stedman, S.M. and J. Hanson. 2000. Habitat Connections: Wetlands, fisheries and economics in the South Atlantic Coastal States. National Oceanic and Atmospheric Administration, National Marine Fisheries Service. http://www.nmfs.noaa.gov/habitat/habitatconservation/publications/habitatconections/num2.htm. Stedman and Hanson.

Stevens, C.E., C.A. Paszkowski, and A.L. Foote. 2007. Beaver (Castor canadensis) as a surrogate species for conserving anuran amphibians on boreal streams in Alberta, Canada. Biological Conservation 134. pp. 1-13.

Stevens, D.L., Jr., and A.R. Olsen. 2004. Spatially-balanced sampling of natural resources. Journal of American Statistical Association. 99:262-278.

Stone, G.W. and C.W. Finkl. eds. 1995. Impacts of Hurricane Andrew on the coastal zones of Florida and Louisiana; August 22–26, 1992. Journal of Coastal Research Special Issue, Vol. 21. 364 p.

Thieler, E.R. and E.S. Hammar-Klose. 1999. National Assessment of Coastal Vulnerability to Sea-Level Rise: Preliminary Results for the U.S. Atlantic Coast. U.S. Geological Survey Open-File Report 99-593, Woods Hole, MA. http://pubs.usgs.gov/of/1999/of99-593/.

Thompson, S.K. 1992. Sampling. John Wiley and Sons, Inc., New York, NY. 343 p.

Turner, R.E., S.W. Forsythe, and N.J. Craig. 1981. Bottomland hardwood forest land resources of the Southeastern United States. In: Wetlands of Bottomland Hardwood Forests. J.R. Clark and J. Benforado. eds. Elsevier, Amsterdam. pp. 13-28.

Twilley, R.R. 2007. Coastal wetlands and global climate change: Gulf coast wetland sustainability in a changing climate. Pew Center on Global Climate Change. 15 p.

Twilley, R.R., E. Barron, H.L. Gholz, M.A. Harwell, R.L. Miller, D.J. Reed, J.B. Rose, E. Siemann, R., G. Wetzel, and R.J. Zimmerman. 2001. Confronting climate change in the Gulf Coast Region: Prospects for sustaining our ecological heritage: A report of the Union of Concerned Scientists and the Ecological Society of America. UCS Publications: Cambridge, MA.

U.S. Department of Agriculture. 2010. Soil and Water Resources Conservation—2011 Appraisal. U.S. Department of Agriculture, Washington, D.C.

U.S. Department of Agriculture. 2007. Bottomland Timber Establishment on Wetlands Initiative. Fact Sheet, Farm Services Agency, Washington, D.C.

U.S. Department of Agriculture, Natural Resources Conservation Service. 2010. On-line resource: http://soils.usda.gov/use/hydric/.

U.S. Department of the Interior 2009. Priority performance goal for climate change mitigation. On-line resource: http://www.doi.gov/budget/2011/11Hilites/DH011.pdf.

U.S. Environmental Protection Agency. 2010a. Coastal Wetlands Initiative: Mid-Atlantic review. U.S. Environmental Protection Agency, Office of Wetlands, Washington, D.C. 22 p.

U.S. Environmental Protection Agency. 2010b. On-line resource: http://water.epa.gov/lawsregs/guidance/wetlands/silv2.cfm.

U.S. Environmental Protection Agency. 2010c. On-line resource: Management Measures for Urban Areas - VIII. Glossary: http://www.epa.gov/owow/NPS/MMGI/Chapter4/ch4-8.html.

U.S. Environmental Protection Agency. 2010d. On-line resource: New Development Management Measure - II. Urban Runoff: http://www.epa.gov/owow/NPS/MMGI/Chapter4/ch4-2a.html.

U.S. Environmental Protection Agency. 2010e. On-line resource: http://water.epa.gov/scitech/climatechange/upload/impacts_on_water_resources.pdf.

U.S. Environmental Protection Agency. 2009. Catalog of federal funding sources for watershed protection. On-line resource: http://cfpub.epa.gov/fedfund/.

U. S. Environmental Protection Agency. 2008. National Coastal Condition Report III. Office of Research and Development/Office of Water EPA/842-R-08-002. Washington, D.C. 295 p.

U.S. Environmental Protection Agency. 2002. Methods for Evaluating Wetland Condition: Using Algae to Assess Environmental Conditions in Wetlands. Office of Water, U.S. Environmental Protection Agency, Washington, DC. EPA-822-R-02-021.

U.S. Environmental Protection Agency. Unpublished. Coastal Wetlands Initiative: South-Atlantic Review. U.S. Environmental Protection Agency, Office of Wetlands, Washington, D.C. 62 p.

U.S. Fish and Wildlife Service. 1980. 660 FW 2, Wetlands Classification System. U.S. Fish and Wildlife Service, Information Resources and Technology Management. On-line reference: http://www.fws.gov/policy/660fw2.html.

U.S. Fish and Wildlife Service. 2010. Rising to the Urgent Challenge Strategic Plan for Responding to Accelerating Climate Change. Washington, D.C.

Watmough, M.D., D.W. Ingstrup, D.C. Duncan, and H.J. Schinke. 2002. Prairie Habitat Joint Venture Habitat Monitoring Program Phase 1: Recent habitat trends in NAWMP targeted landscapes. Technical Report Series No. 391, Canadian Wildlife Service, Edmonton, Alberta, Canada. 93 p.

Webb, P.W. 2008. The impact of changes in water level and human development on forage fish assemblages in Great Lakes coastal marshes. Journal of Great Lakes Research. 34:615–630.

Wear, D.N. and J.G. Greis. eds. 2002. Southern forest resource assessment. Final Report Technical SRS-53. U.S. Department of Agriculture, Forest Service, Southern Research Station. Asheville, NC. 635 p.

Whigham, D.F. 1999. Ecological issues related to wetland preservation, restoration, creation and assessment. The Science of the Total Environment. 240. pp. 31-40.

White, L. and M.B. Martin. 2004. Wildlife in urban landscapes: Use of golf course ponds by wetlands birds. Dept. of Wildlife Ecology and Conservation, FL Coop. Extension Service, Inst. of Food and Agricultural Sciences, Univ. of Florida. http://edis.ifas.ufl.edu.

White, W.A., T.A. Tremblay, R.L.Waldinger, and T.R. Calnan. 2002. Status and trends of wetlands and aquatic habitats on Texas barrier islands, Matagorda Bay to San Antonio Bay. Texas General Land Office and National Oceanic and Atmospheric Administration. 66 p.

Williams, D.R. and K.D. Connolly. 2005. Federal wetlands regulation: An overview. In: K.D. Connolly, S.M. Johnson and D.R. Williams, Wetlands Law and Policy - understanding Section 404. Section of Environment, Energy, and Resources. American Bar Association. pp. 1-26.

Williams, K., K.C. Ewel, R.P. Stumpf, F.E.Putz, and T.W. Workman. 1999. Sea-level rise and coastal forest retreat on the west coast of Florida, USA. Ecology, Vol. 80, No. 6, pp. 2045-2063.

Winter, T. C. 2000. The vulnerability of wetlands to climate change: A hydrologic landscape perspective. J. of the Am. Water Res. Assoc. Vol. 36, Issue 2. pp. 305-311.

Withers, K. 2002. Shorebird use of coastal wetland and barrier island habitat in the Gulf of Mexico. The Scientific World Journal 2:514-536.

Woodcock, T.S., M.C. Monaghan, and K.E. Alexander. 2010. Ecosystem characteristics and summer secondary production in stormwater ponds and reference wetlands. Wetlands, Vol. 30, No. 3. pp. 461-474.

Wolman, H., G. Galster, R. Hanson, M. Ratcliffe, K. Furdell, and A. Sarzynski. 2005. The fundamental challenge in measuring sprawl: Which land should be considered? The Professional Geographer, 57(1). pp. 94-105.

Working Group for Post-Hurricane Planning for the Louisiana Coast. 2006. A new framework for planning the future of Coastal Louisiana after the hurricanes of 2005. University of Maryland, Center for Environmental Science, Cambridge, Maryland. 48 p.

Zedler, J.B. 2006. Wetland Restoration. In: D.P. Batzer and R.R. Sharitz eds. Ecology of Freshwater and Estuarine Wetlands. Univ. of CA Press, Berkeley. pp. 348 -406.

Zinn, J.A. and C. Copeland. 2007. Wetlands: An overview of issues. Congressional Research Service, Report for Congress (RL33483). 20 p.

This page left intentionally blank

Appendix A.
Acknowledgment of Cooperators

The Fish and Wildlife Service is indebted to the following agencies and organizations who have provided services, expertise and assistance over the course of this study.

Alaska Biological Research, Inc.
Environmental Research and Services
Fairbanks, Alaska

Dr. Ken Burnham
Statistician
Dept. of Statistics[28]
Colorado State University
Fort Collins, Colorado

Canadian Wildlife Service
Environmental Conservation Branch
Prairie and Northern Region
Edmonton, Alberta
Canada

Council on Environmental Quality
Washington, D.C.

Ducks Unlimited, Inc.
Great Lakes and Atlantic Regional Office
Ann Arbor, Michigan

Digital Globe Corporation
Longmont, Colorado

GeoEye
Dulles, Virginia

Mr. Rusty Griffin
SWCA Environmental Consultants
Portland, Oregon

L-3 STRATIS
Enterprise Geospatial Solutions
Portland, Oregon

Minnesota Dept. Nat. Resources
St. Paul, Minnesota

Minnesota Dept. Nat. Resources
Forestry/Resource Assessment
Grand Rapids, Minnesota

Natural Resources Assessment Group
University of Massachusetts
Department of Plant & Soil Sciences
Amherst, Massachusetts.

Office of Science Advisor
U.S. Fish and Wildlife Service
Arlington, Virginia

National Oceanic and Atmospheric Administration
National Marine Fisheries Service
Silver Spring, Maryland

Office of Management and Budget
Washington, D.C.

Jeff Powell
Alabama Ecological Services Field Office
U.S. Fish and Wildlife Service
Daphne, Alabama

Denise Rowell
Alabama Ecological Services Field Office
U.S. Fish and Wildlife Service
Daphne, Alabama

South Dakota State University
Department of Wildlife and Fisheries
Brookings, South Dakota

St. Mary's University
Geospatial Services Department
Winona, Minnesota

---

[28] Retired, U.S. Geological Survey, Colorado
Cooperative Fish and Wildlife Research Unit.

Jim Sutherlin, Area Manager
J. D. Murphree WMA
Texas Parks and Wildlife Department
Port Arthur, Texas

Three Parameters, Inc.
Anchorage, Alaska

U.S. Department of Agriculture
Natural Resource Conservation Service
Washington, D.C.
U.S. Army Corps of Engineers
Washington, D.C.

U.S. Department of Agriculture
Farm Services Agency
Washington, D.C.

U.S. Environmental Protection Agency
Office of Research and Development
Gulf Ecology Division
Gulf Breeze, Florida

U.S. Environmental Protection Agency
Office of Research and Development
National Health and Environmental
Effects Research Laboratory,
Western Ecology Division
Corvallis, Oregon

U.S. Environmental Protection Agency
Office of Wetlands
Washington, D.C

U.S. Fish and Wildlife Service
Ecological Services Field Office
Daphne, Alabama
U.S. Fish and Wildlife Service
Alaska Region Office
Anchorage, Alaska

U.S. Fish and Wildlife Service
Fishery Resources Office
Onalaska, Wisconsin

U.S. Fish and Wildlife Service
Region 3 HAPET Office
Fergus Falls, Minnesota

U.S. Fish and Wildlife Service
Upper Mississippi River National
Wildlife and Fish Refuge
Winona, Minnesota

U.S. Geological Survey
Commercial Partnerships Team
National Geospatial Tech. Operations
Rolla, Missouri

U.S. Geological Survey
The National Geospatial Program
Reston, Virginia

Dr. N. Scott Urquhart
Research Scientist
Dept. of Statistics [29]
Colorado State University
Fort Collins, Colorado

Wisconsin Dept. of Nat. Resources
Lakes and Wetlands Section
Bureau of Watershed Management,
Madison, Wisconsin

Wisconsin Water Science Center
U.S. Geological Survey
Middleton, Wisconsin

---

[29] Retired.

Appendix B.
Definitions of Habitat Categories
Used by Status and Trends

Wetlands[30]

In general terms, wetlands were lands where saturation with water was the dominant factor that determined the nature of soil development and the types of plant and animal communities living in the soil and on its surface. The single feature that most wetlands shared was soil or substrate that was at least periodically saturated with or covered by water. Water created severe physiological problems for all plants and animals except those that were adapted for life in water or in saturated soil.

> *Wetlands are lands transitional between terrestrial and aquatic systems where the water table is usually at or near the surface or the land is covered by shallow water. For purposes of this classification wetlands must have one or more of the following three attributes: (1) at least periodically, the land supports predominantly hydrophytes[31], (2) the substrate is predominantly undrained hydric soil[32], and (3) the substrate is non-soil and is saturated with water or covered by shallow water at some time during the growing season of each year.*

The term wetland included a variety of areas that fell into one of five categories: (1) areas with hydrophytes and hydric soils, such as those commonly known as marshes, swamps, and bogs; (2) areas without hydrophytes but with hydric soils—for example, flats where drastic fluctuation in water level, wave action, turbidity, or high concentration of salts may prevent the growth of hydrophytes; (3) areas with hydrophytes but non-hydric soils, such as margins of impoundments or excavations where hydrophytes have become established but hydric soils have not yet developed; (4) areas without soils but with hydrophytes such as the seaweed covered portions of rocky shores; and (5) wetlands without soil and without hydrophytes, such as gravel beaches or rocky shores without vegetation.

Marine System

The marine system consisted of the open ocean overlying the continental shelf and its associated high energy coastline. Marine habitats were exposed to the waves and currents of the open ocean. Salinity exceeded 30 parts per thousand, with little or no dilution except outside the mouths of estuaries. Shallow coastal indentations or bays without appreciable freshwater inflow and coasts with exposed rocky islands that provide the mainland with little or no shelter from wind and waves were also considered part of the marine system because they generally supported a typical marine biota.

Estuarine System

The estuarine system consisted of deepwater tidal habitats and adjacent tidal wetlands that were usually semi-enclosed by land but have been open, partly obstructed, or sporadic access to the open ocean, and in which ocean water was at least occasionally diluted by freshwater runoff from the land. The salinity may periodically have been increased above that of the open ocean by evaporation. Along some low energy coastlines there was appreciable dilution of sea water. Offshore areas with typical estuarine plants and animals, such as red mangroves (*Rhizophora mangle*) and eastern oysters (*Crassostrea virginica*), were also included in the estuarine system.

---

[30] Adapted from Cowardin *et al.* 1979.

[31] Lichvar and Kartesz 2009.

[32] U.S. Department of Agriculture, Natural Resources Conservation Service maintains the list of hydric soils for the United States (U.S. Department of Agriculture, NRCS 2010).

Marine and Estuarine Subsystems

Subtidal   The substrate is continuously submerged by marine or estuarine waters.

Intertidal   The substrate is exposed and flooded by tides. Intertidal includes the splash zone of coastal waters.

Palustrine System   The palustrine (freshwater) system included all nontidal wetlands dominated by trees, shrubs, persistent emergents, emergent mosses or lichens, farmed wetlands, and all wetlands that occurred in tidal areas where salinity due to ocean derived salts is below 0.5 parts per thousand. It also included wetlands lacking vegetation, but with all of the following four characteristics: (1) area less than 20 acres (8 ha); (2) an active wave formed or bedrock shoreline features are lacking; (3) water depth in the deepest part of a basin less than 6.6 feet (2 meters) at low water; and (4) salinity due to ocean derived salts less than 0.5 parts per thousand.

Classes

Unconsolidated Bottom   Unconsolidated bottom includes all wetlands with at least 25 percent cover of particles smaller than stones, and a vegetative cover less than 30 percent. Examples of unconsolidated substrates are: sand, mud, organic material, cobble gravel.

Unconsolidated Shore   Unconsolidated shore has been restricted to the marine and estuarine system and included all wetland habitats, having two characteristics: (1) unconsolidated substrates with less than 30 percent areal cover of vegetation other than pioneering plants.

Emergent Wetland   Emergent wetlands were characterized by erect, rooted, herbaceous hydrophytes, excluding mosses and lichens. This vegetation was present for most of the growing season in most years. These wetlands were usually dominated by perennial plants.

Shrub Wetland   Shrub Wetlands included areas dominated by woody vegetation less than 20 feet (6 meters) tall. The species included true shrubs, young trees, and trees or shrubs that were small or stunted because of environmental conditions.

Forested Wetland   Forested Wetlands were characterized by woody vegetation that was 6 meters tall or taller.

Farmed Wetland   Farmed wetlands were wetlands that met the Cowardin *et al.* definition where the soil surface had been mechanically or physically altered for production of crops, but where hydrophytes would become reestablished if farming was discontinued.

Deepwater Habitats

Wetlands and deepwater habitats were defined separately because the term wetland does not include deep, permanent water bodies. For conducting status and trends studies, riverine and lacustrine were considered deepwater habitats. Elements of marine or estuarine systems can be wetland or deepwater. Palustrine included only wetland habitats.

Deepwater habitats were permanently flooded land lying and included environments where surface water was permanent and often deep, so that water, rather than air, was the principal medium in which the dominant organisms lived, whether or not they were attached to the substrate. As in wetlands, the dominant plants were hydrophytes; however, the substrates were considered nonsoil because the water is too deep to support emergent vegetation.

Riverine System   The riverine system included deepwater habitats contained in a channel, with the exception of habitats with water containing ocean derived salts in excess of 0.5 parts per thousand. A channel was "an open conduit either naturally or artificially created which periodically or continuously contains moving water, or which forms a connecting link between two bodies of standing water" (Langbein and Iseri 1960)..

Lacustrine System   The lacustrine system includes deepwater habitats with all of the following characteristics: (1) situated in a topographic depression or a dammed river channel; (2) lacking trees, shrubs, persistent emergents, emergent mosses or lichens with greater than 30 percent coverage; (3) total area exceeded 20 acres (8 ha).

Uplands

Agriculture[33]   Agricultural land was defined broadly as land used primarily for production of food and fiber. Agricultural activity was evidenced by distinctive geometric field and road patterns on the landscape and the traces produced by livestock or mechanized equipment. Examples of agricultural land use included cropland and pasture; orchards, groves, vineyards, nurseries, cultivated lands, and ornamental horticultural areas including sod farms; confined feeding operations; and other agricultural land including livestock feed lots, farmsteads including houses, support structures (silos) and adjacent yards, barns, poultry sheds, etc.

Urban   Urban land was comprised of areas of intensive use in which much of the land was covered by structures (high building density). Urbanized areas were cities and towns that provide the goods and services needed to survive by modern-day standards through a central business district. Services such as banking, medical, legal office buildings, supermarkets, and department stores made-up the business portion of urban areas. Commercial strip developments along main transportation routes, shopping centers, contiguous dense residential areas, industrial and commercial complexes, transportation, power and communication facilities, city parks, ball fields and golf courses were also included in the urban category.

---

[33] Adapted from Anderson *et al.* 1976.

Forested Plantation   Forested plantations included areas of planted and managed forest stands. Planted pines, Christmas tree farms, clear cuts, and other managed forest stands, such as hardwood forestry were included in this category. Forested plantations were identified by observing the following remote sensing indicators: ((1) trees planted in rows or blocks; (2) forested blocks growing with uniform crown heights; and (3) logging activity and use patterns.

Rural Development   Rural developments occurred in sparse rural and suburban settings outside distinct urban cities and towns and were characterized by non-intensive land use and sparse building density. Typically, a rural development is a cross-roads community that has a corner gas station and a convenience store which are surrounded by sparse residential housing and agriculture. Scattered suburban communities located outside of a major urban center were also included in this category as well as some industrial and commercial complexes; isolated transportation, power, and communication facilities; strip mines; quarries; and recreational areas. Major highways through rural development areas were included in the rural development category.

Other Land Use   Other Land Use was composed of uplands not characterized by the previous categories. Typically these lands included native prairie; unmanaged or non-patterned upland forests and scrub lands; and barren land. Lands in transition were also included in this category. Transitional lands were lands characterized by the lack of any remote sensor information that would enable the analyst to reliably predict future use. The transitional phase occurred when wetlands were drained, ditched, filled, leveled, or the vegetation had been removed and the area was temporarily bare.

Appendix C.
Physiographic Regions of the Conterminous United States as Used in This Study

(adapted from Hammond 1970)

2	Puget-Willamette Lowland
3	Cascade-Klamath-Sierra Nevada Ranges
4	Central Valley of California
5	Columbia Basin
6	Blue Mountains
7	Harney-Owyhee Broken Lands
8	Basin and Range Area
9	Northern Rocky Mountains
10	Snake River Lowland
11	Middle Rocky Mountains
12	Wyoming-Big Horn Basins
13	Colorado River Plateaus
14	Upper Gila Mountains
15	North-Central Lake-Swamp-Moraine Plains
16	Upper Missouri Basin Broken Lands
17	Southern Rocky Mountains

18	Rocky Mountain Piedmont
19	High Plains
20	Stockton-Balcones Escarpment
21	Dakota-Minnesota Drift and Lake-bed Flats
22	Nebraska Sand Hills
23	West-Central Rolling Hills
24	Mid-continent Plains and Escarpments
25	Southwest Wisconsin Hills
26	Middle Western Upland Plain
27	Ozark-Ouachita Highlands

28	Lower Mississippi Alluvial Plain
29	East-Central Drift and Lake-bed Flats
30	Eastern Interior Uplands and Basins
31	Appalachian Highlands
32	Adirondack-New England Highlands
33	Lower New England
34	Gulf-Atlantic Rolling Plain
35	Gulf-Atlantic Coastal Flats
36	Coastal Zone
37	Pacific Coast

Appendix D. Estimates of Acreage by Classification and Change between 2004 and 2009

The rows identify the 2009 classification. The columns identify the classification for 2004. The percent coefficients of variation for estimates appear below the acreage entry[34].

2009 Classification			Marine Subtidal	Marine Intertidal	Estuarine Subtidal	Estuarine Emergents	Estuarine Forested Shrub	Estuarine Unconsolidated Shore	Palustrine Forested	Palustrine Shrub	Palustrine Emergents	Aquaculture Ponds	Agriculture Ponds
			Saltwater Habitats						Freshwater Habitats				
Saltwater Habitats		Marine Subtidal	3,840,393 / 18	3,323 / 60	2,746 / 82	16 / 95	0 / –	172 / 95	0 / –	0 / –	0 / –	0 / –	0 / –
		Marine Intertidal	4,999 / 27	212,959 / 16	65 / 69	0 / –	16 / 96	118 / 95	0 / –	0 / –	0 / –	0 / –	0 / –
		Estuarine Subtidal	15,616 / 60	3,892 / 60	18,634,985 / 8	15,892 / 25	865 / 71	22,384 / 21	0 / –	0 / –	0 / –	0 / –	0 / –
		Estuarine Emergents	1,104 / 52	2,647 / 40	111,171 / 18	8,826,958 / 5	5,627 / 25	21,197 / 21	0 / –	0 / –	0 / –	0 / –	0 / 96
		Estuarine Forested Shrub	150 / 87	599 / 51	1,020 / 27	7,587 / 39	667,847 / 18	605 / 28	0 / –	17 / 96	28 / 92	0 / –	2 / 96
		Estuarine Unconsolidated	6,907 / 55	1,154 / 42	18,808 / 20	5,007 / 26	1,404 / 37	969,633 / 14	0 / –	0 / –	0 / 0	0 / –	0 / –
Freshwater Habitats		Palustrine Forested	0 / –	0 / –	4 / 96	215 / 93	1,201 / 99	0 / –	50,521,113 / 3	774,774 / 13	474,416 / 10	50 / 100	15,436 / 18
		Palustrine Shrub	0 / –	385 / 97	0 / –	416 / 62	327 / 80	133 / 54	1,028,027 / 14	16,786,447 / 4	206,954 / 14	77 / 99	8,949 / 22
		Palustrine Emergents	0 / –	659 / 95	2,633 / 78	1,805 / 94	261 / 98	2,002 / 87	53,363 / 18	777,550 / 9	25,410,396 / 8	625 / 79	44,712 / 21
		Aquaculture Ponds	0 / –	0 / –	0 / –	0 / –	0 / –	8 / 95	0 / –	4,125 / 43	43,750 / 45	250,211 / 35	449 / 63
		Agriculture Ponds	0 / –	33 / 99	0 / –	0 / –	0 / –	0 / –	558 / 100	7,231 / 29	70,688 / 34	1,111 / 79	2,668,660 / 4
		Industrial Ponds	0 / –	0 / –	18 / 71	72 / 98	0 / –	0 / –	0 / –	875 / 42	5,502 / 36	0 / –	0 / –
		Natural Ponds	0 / –	0 / –	148 / 54	146 / 96	0 / –	0 / –	1,683 / 99	24,170 / 13	100,201 / 9	124 / 98	3,116 / 36
		Urban Ponds	0 / –	0 / –	101 / 95	106 / 98	21 / 98	0 / –	0 / –	1,664 / 27	15,488 / 26	0 / –	12,788 / 21
Deepwater Habitats		Lacustrine	0 / –	0 / –	7,186 / 83	0 / –	27 / 96	28 / 94	0 / –	8,770 / 40	118,481 / 27	8,555 / 91	1,048 / 70
		Riverine	0 / –	0 / –	362 / 87	0 / –	0 / –	0 / –	728 / 98	12,788 / 37	11,074 / 32	0 / –	1,203 / 96
Uplands		Agriculture	0 / –	0 / –	29 / 96	62 / 98	129 / 96	0 / –	772 / 88	69,716 / 35	581,345 / 20	9,725 / 54	132,598 / 8
		Urban	0 / –	0 / –	188 / 77	110 / 78	0 / –	0 / –	0 / –	1,292 / 63	18,578 / 43	0 / –	420 / 84
		Other	502 / 45	2,050 / 37	1,685 / 19	1,398 / 38	2,185 / 66	1,363 / 28	18,126 / 42	33,260 / 28	347,764 / 39	243 / 60	81,793 / 28
		Forested Plantation	0 / –	0 / –	0 / –	0 / –	0 / –	11 / 71	3,780 / 32	7,817 / 40	16,329 / 38	165 / 59	6,460 / 17
		Rural Development	0 / –	58 / 94	375 / 63	58 / 98	0 / –	45 / 82	246 / 91	1,001 / 54	14,524 / 28	271 / 53	3,266 / 30
Acreage Totals, 2009			3,869,671 / 18	227,759 / 15	18,776,475 / 8	8,859,839 / 5	679,909 / 12	1,017,692 / 18	51,628,347 / 3	18,511,498 / 4	27,480,470 / 8	266,157 / 33	2,980,849 / 4

[34] Palustrine farmed has not been reported as a separate category. Palustrine farmed acreage was included in the appropriate classification/land use type.

Percent Coefficient of Variation

Industrial Ponds	Natural Ponds	Urban Ponds	Lacustrine	Riverine	Agriculture	Urban	Other	Forested Plantation	Rural Development	Acreage Totals, 2004	
			Deepwater Habitats		Uplands						
0	0	0	0	0	0	0	40	0	0	3,846,690	Marine Subtidal
–	–	–	–	–	–	–	76	–	–	18	
0	0	0	0	0	0	0	1,089	0	0	219,246	Marine Intertidal
–	–	–	–	–	–	–	54	–	–	15	
1	0	0	61	0	0	335	829	0	567	18,695,426	Estuarine Subtidal
94	–	–	85	–	–	66	37	–	76	3	
25	0	8	8	0	20	881	2,059	19	166	8,971,885	Estuarine Emergents
94	–	52	95	–	71	40	29	94	46	5	
68	0	5	0	0	35	975	204	0	164	679,307	Estuarine Forested Shrub
86	–	96	–	–	67	67	65	–	64	12	
0	0	128	0	0	0	126	1,215	0	11	999,389	Estuarine Unconsolidated
–	–	95	–	–	–	51	88	–	94	14	
2,015	16,236	9,441	7,130	8,864	78,073	50,886	91,628	158,224	51,750	52,256,455	Palustrine Forested
58	24	28	62	41	17	18	26	20	19	3	
3,205	15,618	4,952	15,480	6,799	41,928	21,654	17,520	150,440	27,180	18,331,440	Palustrine Shrub
54	28	22	44	41	16	25	29	28	32	4	
5,071	62,679	16,458	123,268	4,062	582,075	26,269	29,909	44,857	24,064	27,162,705	Palustrine Emergents
40	14	18	18	49	18	15	26	55	17	8	
0	0	756	0	0	71,026	2,682	5,485	1,924	305	880,720	Aquaculture Ponds
–	–	80	–	–	34	78	60	99	78	28	
1,296	1,042	7,509	8,388	0	36,823	600	7,675	7,024	9,840	2,828,473	Agriculture Ponds
85	69	36	49	–	25	39	46	65	51	4	
345,818	97	910	8,282	0	57	2,849	5,209	288	8,944	378,370	Industrial Ponds
18	98	28	58	–	71	56	85	71	45	17	
2,115	1,952,844	2,832	5,070	259	4,680	522	8,789	149	2,200	2,103,499	Natural Ponds
48	12	87	82	95	41	29	84	79	42	11	
694	1,395	765,671	1,749	0	686	9,124	8,584	1,150	1,942	816,063	Urban Ponds
75	51	6	64	–	58	26	41	100	36	6	
481	5,127	101	16,619,680	0	1,626	8,575	6,898	866	14,125	16,786,019	Lacustrine
80	31	68	10	–	50	51	48	88	78	10	
1	5,295	320	796	7,482,451	317	31	2,571	0	0	7,517,985	Riverine
99	86	98	81	9	98	99	49	–	–	9	
11,696	13,219	46,104	29,451	3,435							Agriculture
39	29	15	30	56							
1,481	189	32,364	3,685	0							Urban
47	45	20	52	–							
17,831	10,832	42,066	24,978	4,541							Other
26	19	22	42	54							
1,206	3,415	12,555	5,629	0							Forested Plantation
47	49	33	67	–							
17,959	1,805	20,849	10,950	121							Rural Development
26	63	19	43	99							
410,462	2,088,798	968,019	16,859,594	7,510,581							Acreage Totals, 2009
16	11	6	10	9							

U.S. Department of the Interior
U.S. Fish & Wildlife Service

http://www.fws.gov

September 2011

Cover photograph: Freshwater wetlands, Wyoming, 2010.